Glossator: Practice an[illegible]

Volume 3

GLOSSATOR

Practice and Theory of the Commentary

VOLUME 3

http://glossator.org

ISSN 1942-3381 (online)
ISSN 2152-1506 (print)

Questions may be directed to:

Nicola Masciandaro, Editor
Glossator: Practice and Theory of the Commentary
Department of English
Brooklyn College, The City University of New York
2900 Bedford Ave.
Brooklyn, NY 11210
glossatori@gmail.com

[Cover image by Karl Steel]

Glossator 3: Open-Topic (2010)

CONTENTS

THE *NIGHT VIGIL* OF SHEN ZHOU

J. H. Prynne

On a cold night sleep is very sweet. I woke in the middle of the night, my mind clear and untroubled, and as I was unable to go to sleep again, I put on my clothes and sat facing my flickering lamp. On the table were a few folders of books. I chose a volume at random and began to read, but tiring I put down the book and sat calmly doing nothing [*shushou weizuo*]. A long rain had newly cleared, and a pale moon was shining through the window. All around was silence.

Then after a long time absorbing the fresh brightness, I gradually became aware of sounds. Listening to the rustling of the wind stirring the bamboo gave one the feeling of going bravely and unwaveringly onward. Hearing the harsh snarling of dogs gave feelings of barring out evil, of opposing marauders. Hearing the sound of drums, large and small–the small ones thin, and the far ones clear and deep and uninterrupted–stirred restless thoughts that were lonely and sad. The official drum was very close, from three beats, to four and then five, gradually faster, hastening the dawn. Suddenly in the northeast the sound of a bell, a bell pure and clean through rain-cleared air, and hearing it came thoughts of waiting for the dawn, rising and doing. It was inevitable.

My nature is such as to enjoy sitting in the night [*yezuo*]. So I often spread a book under the lamp going back and forth over it, usually stopping at the second watch. Man's clamor is not at rest, and yet the mind is bent on learning. Seldom does he find the outside calm and the inner world at peace [*wai jing er nei ding*].

Now tonight all sounds and shapes [*shengse*] bring this stability and calm [*dingjing*]. Thus can one purify the mind [*xin*] and spirit [*shen*] and realize one's will [*zhiyi*]. But one should remember that it is not that at other times these sounds and shapes do not exist like this, nor that they do not reach the eye and ear of man, but that appearance is the servant of a thing, and yet the mind hastens to follow it.

True perception through hearing [*cong*] lies concealed in sound like that of drum and bell [*kenghong*], whereas perception through seeing [*ming*] is hidden in any pattern [*wenhua*]. Thus things usually harm rather than help men. Often is it like tonight's sounds and shapes, for they are really no different from other times, and yet striking the ear and eye they become so firmly [*liran*] and wonderfully a part of me. And so this existence of sounds and patterns is not what prevents me from gaining wisdom; for things are [not] enough to enslave men.

When sound is broken and shape shattered and the will [*zhi*] rises free, what is this will? Is it within? Or is it without? Or is it in a thing? Or does it cause the thing to be? Is there not a way of defining the difference? Most certainly, and I perceive the difference.

How great is the strength to be gained sitting in the night. Thus, cleansing the mind, waiting alone through the long watches by the light of a newly trimmed bright candle becomes the basis of an inner peace and of an understanding of things. This, surely, will I attain.

I made this record of a night vigil in 1492 during the autumn on the sixteenth day of the seventh month. Shen Chou of Suzhou.

SHEN CHOU (modern pinyin SHEN ZHOU) of Suzhou (1425-1509), inscribed holograph colophon to his hanging scroll-painting 'Night Vigil'; translated text here from Richard Edwards, *The Field of Stones; A Study of the Art of Shen Chou (1427-1509)* (Washington, D.C., 1962), p. 57; for another fuller account see James Cahill, *Parting at the Shore; Chinese Painting of the Early and Middle Ming Dynasty, 1368-1580* (New York, 1978), pp. 90-91 and plates 37-8 (monochrome reproduction); for an extended and recent investigation also see Kathlyn Maurean Liscomb, 'The Power of Quiet Sitting at Night: Shen Zhou's (1427-1509) Night Vigil', *Monumenta Serica*, 43 (1995), 381-403 (I have inserted her transcription of certain Chinese terms into the Edwards text, above; also, the 'not' in square brackets [para.

5] is inserted here because she records textual evidence that a character is probably missing and is probably bu, 'not'). Poor-quality colour reproduction in *Ninety Years of Wu School Painting* (Taipei, 1975), p. 2, or <http://www.123soho.com/artgroup/national_palace_museum /1000/np_4ex4.htm>. The *Monumenta Serica* publication includes a good black-and-white reproduction plus detailed enlargement of the colophon and also of the picture-area (figs 1-3, pp. 393-5). Best internet images (b&w), which allow enlargement and zoom into detail with good resolution, are mounted in the Huntington Archive of Buddhist and Related Art, available online at <http://huntington.wmc.ohio-state.edu/public/> – here click on 'search or browse the archive' then in search box enter 'night vigil' and click on SEARCH.

Shen Zhou (in modern pinyin) was one of the exemplary and renowned major painter-calligraphers of the fifteenth-century Wu school that developed in the Suzhou area of central China, a little to the west of what is now Shanghai; for more information about this school see Susan Bush, *The Chinese Literati on Painting: Su Shih (1037-1101) to Tung Sh'i-ch'ang (1555-1636)* (Cambridge, Mass., 1971), pp. 172-9, Sherman E. Lee, *Chinese Landscape Painting* (2nd rev. ed., New York, 1962), pp. 65-82, and James Cahill, *Parting at the Shore*, Chap. 2. This prose text is translated into English by Edwards from the artist's colophon, the inscribed upper portion of a painted scroll known as 'Night Vigil', ink and slight colours on paper, 84.8 x 21.8 cm, dated to the Hung-chih era, jen-tzu year [i.e., 1492], and now in the National Palace Museum, Taipei (ROC), with seals of Shen Zhou and others. This text in translation is also supplied in part, with comments, by Cahill (*Parting at the Shore*, p. 90), and more fully retranslated by Liscomb (my critical comments on some of her points should not obscure the many benefits I have derived from her full discussion).

The (lower) picture-area shews a small settlement of simple open-sided shelters (maybe not quite pavilions), nestled within a group of scattered pine trees rising up from sloping rough terrain at the foot of high mountain peaks, with a modest plank foot-bridge in the foreground leading across a mountain stream into the secluded central focus (on the plank-bridge motif see Esther Jacobson-Leong, 'Place and Passage in the Chinese Arts: Visual Images and Poetic Analogues', *Critical Enquiry*, 3 [1976], 345-368 [pp. 355, 358]; for a similar device compare T'ang Yin's *The Cottage in Bamboo Forest* and his *Wu Yangzi Nourishing His Nature* [both Palace Museum, Taibei]).

The ultra-tall pine trees, somewhat out of naturalistic perspective, rise from the ground level of the shelters, right up through the mist, apparently (by foreshortening) to the level of the mountains behind or at least their lower flanks; no doubt the near presence of the stream-water makes their footing moist and fertile (the pair of trees to the right may be broad-leaved, but those on the left are stylised conifers according to tradition). An allegorist might say, thought aspires upwards like these elongated tall trees, bare of lower branches; but trees thus hemmed in by permanent shadow from major landforms do of course always in response develop a characteristically taller habit. It's in their nature to behave as if like allegory, just as their actual long-lived species habit gained for them the iconic symbolism of human longevity.

There, beneath a layer of hovering misty vapour, precipitated by the cooling of moisture-bearing air after sundown, and within the central shelter (perhaps close to a traditional study-pavilion according to custom), sits the upright solitary scholar in meditation-posture on his low dais or *kang*, arms folded as the mark of bodily inaction, his books beside him on the table which also supports the candle-holder: a diminutive self-figure whose inner mind is fully disclosed in this outward scene, the interior of his shelter bright from the single candle, all held in motionless contemplation. (Kathlyn Liscomb refers to this light structure as 'a bucolic villa' [p. 396], wrong both as description and also in tone.) For a contemporary example of another reclusive mountain pavilion compare T'ang Yin's *Scholar in a Pavilion of circa 1499-1502*, borrowing many features of Shen Zhou's style (Palace Museum, Taibei; see Anne de Coursey Clapp, *The Painting of T'ang Yin* [Chicago, 1991], pp. 117-20 & fig. 38).

Here in Shen Zhou's painting the scholar's books lie on the table beside him but he is not looking at or towards them. He comments that 'the mind is bent on learning' and yet he chooses a book at random, this is not part of any plan of study: the learning sought after is supported by reading but is not to be won principally from books. The light from the inside candle marks a bright radiance of the heart/mind: that of the moon outside, a diffused luminous enhancement of natural appearance; this part-match in two kinds of light/enlightenment sets up a correspondence which is here also a problematic question. He has his back to the mountains which are not in his immediate field of view, even were the moon bright enough to allow them to be glimpsed at least in profile; they are part of his familiar inward knowledge of companionable forms, in the general darkness outside, rather than visible to him as they are to us: we need to see what he already knows.

The tying of the reclusive scholar's top-knot playfully echoes the form of the thatched kiosk-roof behind him, which is maybe bright towards the apex because catching and reflecting light from the moon. The band of mist segregates the towering peaks from direct connection with the world of men, below; and further above is the third upper layer, of the text-space, inscribed downwards as reverse match for the upward movement of the ascending landscape. Above the highest mountain peak, in this upper text-area, is this unusually extensive colophon, a composed but half-spontaneous essay arising directly from the moment shewn in the picture, taking up some one-third of the complete picture format: this is the expressed mind-space of the whole composition. The mountain peaks are essential wilderness, within and beyond which meditation (Daoist, Chan-Buddhist, neo-Confucian) has traditionally belonged.

At first the absorbed self is immune to outer sound, but then his senses sharpen and he hears natural sounds or noises that come deeply into consciousness; as silence is restored, he ponders the connection between outward and inward perception, in relation to the formation of human resolve. Liscomb comments thus: 'Shen's essay conveys the belief that the existence of principle in everything enables people to experience a marvelous union with the things in their environment, as long as selfish desires do not distort or obscure their perceptions. Without such a belief in such an underlying unity, the link of human convictions and concerns with sounds made by plants, animals, and musical instruments would be considered by most people to be incidental or arbitrary' (p. 390).

But this is to separate the enquiring mode of speculative thinking from the art and insights of the painter. The scene depicted does indeed shew the human mind in nature as a central informing presence, preoccupied with central questions of traffic between subjective and objective reality and the priorities for human character and resolved action. But also it represents the material world itself, of both nature and man, as placed in the structure of a substantial landscape however idealised: the shelters are stationed where they are because the ledge in the lower part of the mountains is level and can support these informal dwelling-places, defended by trees and bushes, as neighbourhood forms, from wild winds and driving rain. The communal spaces around the shelters look to be neatly swept, as is of course to be expected. Even if the towering peaks owe almost everything to generic image-ideas and profiles, within the tradition, the vernacular foreground of broken rocks and scree and vegetation is grounded in a reality not of the mind, but handled with affectionate regard for how such things are: too rough and stony for cultivation of crops but within reach of a close sympathy for the tones and formal contrasts of surface and its overt presence in the scheme of place. The treatment of this foreground is ethically principled, deeply attested by the plank bridge, and is intimate with the central purposes of the colophon essay.

The rustic plank bridge is thus not a formal, built structure, it is a 'natural' expedient, by well-established convention providing human access to this retired 'place' of nature: the mountain stream as here a modest barrier to man is also the expression of moisture as a need of all living things, and the plank is from a tree that had grown to maturity by advantage from this moisture. What flows and what remains still: the plank crosses the running stream but is supported by the firmness of the solid banks on either side, signaling the near and the far, the water descending from higher ground: the primal dimensions of being in space. The understated eloquence of this pathway for the viewer to enter this scene, to visit the human community within the small settlement beyond the bridge, resides in the simple, informal matching of art to nature, art hewn from nature to extend art's naturalised domain. As 'honoured guest' the viewer is invited by this visible link to follow the track which is a daily passage for those regularly using it. The bridge is just wide enough for a single person; no grand chariots or commercial wagons shall have business here.

Many traditional village settlements in rural settings would routinely have been fortified and gated, to provide protection against bandits, but here the prospect is innocent of defensive anxiety. The painter trusts the viewer, and we sense this from his serious, hospitable openness, the view unimpeded by darkness or gates or window coverings. Thus, the plank bridge conducts us directly into the disclosed inner heart-mind of the vigil itself. It is a spirit bridge, crafted out of solid timber.

Liscomb comments again, 'Shen employs semi-abstracted landscape forms to serve as metaphors for the moral resolve and thoughts aroused by various sounds of the night. Also, because the sounds came from things in his surrounding environment, using highly charged landscape forms to evoke his determined responses is an effective way to convey his marvelous union with those things by means of his unobscured senses' (p. 396). This also cannot be right, or not the whole story, because for the painter the status of indeterminate passage-work in the treatment of foreground slopes and bushes, the light drawing-in of the tiles and shingles of the shelter roofing, the easy but attentive account of the channel cut down by the flowing water, are none of them mere metaphors: they are how the world is, of how this picture's composition derives seriously from the composure of human and natural place disclosed here. Little has been done to separate this group of vernacular shelters from the natural components of the mountain scene: the settlement is not enclosed by a gated fence, not much of the undergrowth has been cleared, the whole dwelling idiom is informal and even a shade precarious.

Indeed there is a visual community of forms and links. The rippling lateral rhythm of the roof-coverings speaks by echo of pattern to the running turbulence of the stream over its rocky bed, whose fresh clear water meets the domestic needs of the nearby dwellings, as the painter's brush washes onto the paper the moist smooth tints from his inkstone. If the scene carries meaning it's not by a scheme of representation but through a practice of observance and brushed-in sense of present things; if some of the rising upgrowth behind the main shelter is in fact bamboo, then the free-sketch treatment is in marked contrast to meticulous rendering of the bamboo forms by 'professional' artists, since for the scholar-painter, painting bamboo was, in Sherman Lee's phrase, 'a final test of brushwork' (*Chinese Landscape Painting*, p. 57). What is looked for is quite other, some sense of simplicity in which by conscious choice the art is not artful.

This theme of the painterly as non-subservient can be found as a thread in later aesthetic practice. Jonathan Hay discusses the 'Marbled Stone Cliff' page of the *Eight Views of the South* by Shitao (also known as Daoji, 1642-1707), an album in the British Museum, London, which carries a poem by the painter (probably written at the end of the 1670's) inscribed over a landscape containing, up on the mountain slope, another pavilion with open window-space within which can just be made out a solitary reflective figure; the inscribed poem is explicit in melancholy retrospect, revisiting the site of earlier memories as night pales into dawn:

> I have long missed Taibai's pavilion
> Now that I'm here again, I suddenly grow melancholy.
> The pristine moon of past and present
> Looks down sagely on autumn in the world.

> The Three Mountains opposite seem to sit on the window ledge
> Five drumbeats from the edge of the city mark the dawn.
> Tomorrow I'll be gone, a thousand *li* away
> Looking back on the water's fast current.

And yet despite this assertion of an apparently controlling nostalgia, Hay comments on how 'the painting resists reduction to this metaphoric reading through the filter of the poem' (Jonathan Hay, *Shitao: Painting and Modernity in Early Qing China* [Cambridge, 2001]), p. 311 and fig. 210; his translation). Haun Saussy has in his *The Problem of a Chinese Aesthetic* (Stanford, Cal., 1993) notably extended the discussion of metaphor and allegory in Chinese thought, and in his chapter 1, 'The Question of Chinese Allegory' he argues strongly against the kind of concept-classification which takes metaphor as the link which resolves difference by turning it to use, generative of signification. Citing Pauline Yu, *The Reading of Imagery in the Chinese Poetic Tradition* (Princeton, N.J., 1987) he comments:

> The solidarity between ontology and literary theory, as Yu sees both being traditionally practiced in the West, is complete. Allegory "creates a hierarchical literary universe of two levels, each of which maintains its own coherence, but only one of which has ultimate primacy (Yu, p. 19). Both metaphor and allegory are two instances of an omnipresent law, that of mimesis or fictionality: "Mimesis is . . . predicated on a fundamental ontological dualism–the assumption that there is a truer reality transcendent to the concrete, historical realm in which we live, and that the relation between the two is replicated in the creative act and artifact" (Yu, p. 5) (Saussy, pp. 24-5).

The parallel with Shen Zhou's 'Night Vigil' will suggest that the two juxtaposed modes (pictorial and discursive) comprise an allegorical hybrid, in which the textual is mounted above the scenic, the strong meaning of the first ('higher') controlling and directing the weaker presence ('lower') of the second. This ignores the evident fact that Shen Zhou was first and foremost a painter, not a philosopher or essayist or even poet; his habit of thought is deeply visual and his ethical convictions find and reveal their primary evidence in his paintings, in his consistent treatment of what he sees and his priorities of regard. Is the picture then, in 'Night Vigil', the controlling primary discourse? Again the answer must be 'no' or rather, this question too is ill-formed. The category-difference between painting and speculative autobiography is demonstrated as a kind of reciprocal parity, or each as metaphor/allegory for the other, each explicit in different ways as provided for in the medium, leaving the reader/viewer with the task of a deepened apprehension enhanced by seeing through reading and reading through seeing. Each mode involves recognising a self-reference and also escaping from it: the self-conscious mind is present in the narrative of thought and feeling as expressed in the grammar of language; but the pictorial also has its own grammar, in which the viewer must be practised if the scene is not to be misread or downgraded to subordinate status.

Thus, Shen Zhou's shaggy foliage dots and hatchings are recognisably derived from standard painterly treatments of such landscape components, and yet they demonstrate also a chosen abstinence from neatness; the shaggy stipple climbs right up the far mountain peaks in a confident disregard of distance-perspective. To speak of these features as 'the pleasantly awkward quality of the painted forms' (Liscomb, p. 399) is to notice a characteristic and then rather completely to miss its point. Shen Zhou asks himself this (for him) quite urgent question, very ardently, in his essay: when the will rises free of externally perceived order in sound and sight, what is this will, is it in a thing, or does it cause the thing to be? These shaggy ink-forms are a latent but strong part of the answer: they are in the thing seen and known, just as the movements of brush and ink (*bimo*) cause them to be there on the paper and in the field of view, known in and through the construction of where they are. This is not to solve an ancient problem but to find energy and moral definition in bringing this problem to renewed life. Thus, 'pleasantly awkward' has to be a long way wide of the painterly commitment to a de-commissioning of sophisticated technique, as an ethical principle fully recognised as such in the essay-text.

As viewers we recognise that the social practice implicit in this scene is not that of a fully inhabited village-type settlement, these in-formal structures are more like summer lodges than year-round family homes. They are lightly constructed, and lightly sketched. And yet the barking dogs remind distinctly enough of the need to protect a domestic community from hostile attack, and the regular official drum-beats through the watches of the night confirm that social time is sequenced and marked in this public way. If the clear-striking bell is from a temple, then this too is another kind of community sounding out its spirit-presence in habitable space. (For another night vigil punctuated by drum-beats see Du Fu, 'Ge ye' ['Night at West House'], composed c.766; David Hawkes, *A Little Primer of Tu Fu* [Oxford, 1967], pp. 181-4.)

We recognise also the divided condition of a literary 'pastoral' mode, since the sophistication of the scholar's books and thoughts is not quite naturally at home in this simple rustic environment; his window-space is fully open (it must still be summer weather) to take in a wide view, whereas across the windows of the other shelters there appear to be crossed drapes or curtains; thus, his wakefulness must be in contrast to the natural sleep of those whose day-work has made them tired; so that there is maybe a task to reconcile one rhythm and way of life with the other, through admitting fully the separate categories of reality and being-in-the-world, searching out what may reveal the links across this difference. Perhaps such links or bridges can be profoundly simple, like the informal plank over the stream; but perhaps such simplicity is not easily grasped by a complex mind. Allegory would just be a short cut, intrinsically shallow. In the larger background we recognise also the contrasts of absolute and local temporality; these rocks and mountains have been in existence long before the first men walked the earth, even if continuingly eroded and shaped by weather and climate change; but these trees and bushes have a shorter span, and some of the minor vegetation will be merely seasonal and transient. Thus 'place' is made up of many inherently contradictory elements, even disregarding the perceptual categories brought to it by differences of human and social frequentation.

The scholar-painter will depend on this sense of community as brought to him by these sounds at night because, even if he's clearly a privileged member of the literati class, he is supported by his human environment and he is not detached from the overt reality of small things, not merely wrapped up into metaphors of heart/mind. What he sees is the world that stands and counts for him, before what he thinks, and his understanding lies somewhere between these modalities. So much in Shen Zhou's career as a painter of informal notebook (album) scenes, treated with deep affection like the domestic texture of a natural order, stands as testimony to his non-subscription to allegory as a master trope.

The relations here are, then, not overall those of illustration, nor of allegory or symbolic equivalence, nor yet of distinguishment or separation through resemblance and its iconography; however much traditional classifications may propose otherwise, and even though these category-aspects all do have some specific roles to play. Neither working mode, discursive or pictorial, is secondary to the other. The writing is not on the picture nor even quite in the picture; it is integrally an expressed component of the whole idea and its trace, planned for in dividing up the paper-surface and no doubt done using the same brushes and the same ink (we may note in passing that the writing-style is by no means elegant, but rapid and unlaboured, like a letter or journal). Thus earth and heaven are zonally distinct, and yet their unity is both assumed and also deeply in question. The limited colour-tints are very muted, the overall tonal range quite shadowed, as suits the night-time scene: again Cahill comments, 'Night and moonlight are suggested in the painting only by the paleness of color in some parts and a slight darkening in others' (p. 91). The idiom is Shen Zhou's deceptively informal and relaxed late manner; the whole composition is extremely delicate and sensitive to its own inwardly alert and resonant atmosphere, not at all regulated by fastidiousness as in Ni Tsan (Ni Zan) and others. On this painting Cahill comments, further:

> While Shen Chou does not specifically relate these meditations to the process of artistic creation, it is probably not unwarranted to use them to illuminate his beliefs, and those of Ming literati artists in general, on the relationship between external phenomena and one's experience of them–or, by extension, perceived images in nature and the transformation of them in art. Sensory stimuli are in themselves too bewilderingly diverse, press upon the consciousness too constantly and demandingly, to be absorbed fully by the mind or represented in their raw state in art. The literati artists' continual insistence that verisimilitude, "form likeness," is not their aim is based on a conviction that attempts to represent the world as it appears miss the point; realism in art does not truly reflect human experience of the world, or understanding of it; and it is that experience and understanding they mean to convey–insofar as they choose to engage themselves, as artists, with nature at all. At moments of extraordinary clarity, when the mind is receptive but at rest, uncluttered by distracting considerations–moments such as Shen Chou records so movingly here–one's perceptions become a part of one's

> self, in an undifferentiated "passage of felt life." The cumulative absorption and ordering of such perceptions is the "self-cultivation" of the Confucian system, and this in turn is the proper stuff of art (pp. 90-91).

For the arguments against "form-likeness" or commonplace naturalism in depicting external appearances see James Cahill, *The Lyric Journey; Poetic Painting in China and Japan* (Cambridge, 1996), pp. 73-80. It is probably correct to add also that the habits of thought and perception latent in the 'Night Vigil' text reveal a distinct influence of Daoist/Buddhist attitudes to the seclusion of mind in nature, following the true Way by meditative practice and the suppression of assertive self-agency; though Liscomb prefers to connect these features more with neo-Confucian practice and ideas. Wen Fong comments on how 'the literary Taoists, men of intellectual achievement and great influence, combined Neo-Taoist metaphysical thought with Confucian learning. As friends and companions of leading scholars and artists, they infused the Chiang-nan literati culture with Taoist mysticism, which served as the underlying philosophy for reclusive living. Several literary Taoists were also accomplished painters' (Wen C. Fong, *Beyond Representation; Chinese Painting and Calligraphy, 8th-14th Century* [New Haven, Conn., 1992], p. 470); compare also Anne de Coursey Clapp, *The Painting of T'ang Yin*, pp. 17-24, for an outline reconstruction of T'ang Yin's 'syncretic beliefs'. Marc F. Wilson comments regarding Shen Zhou's poem-colophon to his 'Landscape in the Style of Ni Tsan' of 1484: 'Shen's poem is essentially a summary evaluation of his life and his place in a Confucian society that set a premium on official service and on historical and literary learning. The self-deprecatory tone rests in Taoist alternatives of withdrawal and personal cultivation' (*Eight Dynasties of Chinese Painting; The Collections of the Nelson Gallery-Atkins Museum, Kansas City, and the Cleveland Museum of Art* [Cleveland, Ohio, 1980], p. 179). Richard Edwards comments, also:

> These ideas may spring from Buddhist concepts–and certainly Shen Chou pictures himself seated like a Buddhist sage in his shelter–this stands as a kind of artist's creed. For as the artist must fundamentally deal with matter, the creation or moulding of matter in terms of sounds and shapes, these cannot be considered irrelevant; they are not mere illusion. Rather, all appearance, all manifestations of

> matter, all "things" hold the core of truth. It is through acceptance rather than denial of the world that one learns the nature of reality. Most particularly in these later years Shen Chou paints against a background such as this. For one can see in his scrolls a marvelous balance between the obligation to paint the beauty of the world as it appears to the eye and the necessity to suggest its fragile and deceptive quality as mere appearance. He thus would lead us to its inner and essential nature, to "an understanding of things" (*The Field of Stones*, p. 57).

Such fundamental questions may be approached alternatively by closer attention to paradoxes of temporality. The double presence of visual image and its intimately related text-essay prompts strongly the question of the time frame or time flow for this scroll. The completed physical production by the artist hangs motionless before the viewer: yet to absorb the picture, as also to read the essay, prolongs our encounter in real time. The scene presented is quite still, motionless: the human figure is in alert posture but also relaxed and serene, without need of physical movement: yet the thought-process reported in the stages of the essay is exploring and testing ideas and feelings, traversing a sequence of questions about experience, inward and outward reality. Consciousness is steady and unhurried, but by no means static. The passage through almost-dark night as a linkage of solitary waking hours towards dawn makes a contrast with the closed window-coverings of the other small shelters, where we may suppose other human beings to be at rest and asleep. Theirs will be the shared social activity of the day-time world.

The composition of the time frame is thus pointedly ambiguous, indeed this ambiguity is the notional 'place' of this whole enterprise. Outside the mind of the singular thinker who is also the artist making the external image of this suspended moment, the mountains represent forms that are permanent and enduring: the force for existence of nature prior to man, that will outlast mere human presence. Shen Zhou is, at the instant of his essay, about 67 years old, not a young man but with his own sense of accumulated selfhood. The season is autumn and, as winter approaches, these upland shelters will probably soon be exchanged for more permanent and weather-proof dwellings down below. The tall pine trees remind the viewer of their traditional reference to lasting age; but the more small-scale foliage is seasonal and transitory, the stream flows continuously, downwards to the fertile rice fields that will nourish the artist-thinker; the sounds that punctuate the silence also calibrate the felt lapse of time. Growing insight into ideas that are true can partake of a permanence in truth itself: but thinking and searching in mind and revolving uncertain questions are within the flux of experience, and comprise it. What is the form of all these contradictions and complimentarities about time and duration, permanent and relative, within the self and yet also outside and beyond it? The underlying tacit form is that of mortal life itself, vital principle in all things, joining the human and non-human and even the apparently non-living, within the order of nature and the fluent activity of heart-mind.

This is a conjoint image of what we are to recognise and ourselves experience as The Way, ever-changing in appearance and yet also ever-constant in latent presence for those who can discover its power. The power of undistracted self-understanding, searched for in this essay and latently visible in the pictorial image, confers strength of will, to resolve doubts in aligning individual purpose with The Way and its immanent directive guidance. Once again, the representation here is not allegory or even symbolism: the viewer/reader of this scroll is within the scene and its vigilance and yet of course out of it, just as the meditative human figure (almost but not quite our proxy) is within the natural and human place all around him and yet, also of course, out of it.

It would not be wrong, across cultures, to think of Coleridge's somewhat similar meditative night-piece poem, 'Frost at Midnight' of 1798, another intimate vigil within a darkened landscape; except that Shen Zhou's painting together with its essay-text can set up a dialogue, if not an enquiry, in wider dimensions; reaching deep into questions of human character about how the self is formed, what gives it strength and truth to principle, what is to be learned and understood from what we know of the outer world and its reality, coming into thought through the eye and brush: what that is and how we come to know it rightly and truly.

This way of thinking may be considered in relation to the brief summary by David Hawkes of the philosophical opening ideas of the *Hong Lou Meng* (*The Story of the Stone* (*The Dream of the Red Chamber*]): 'The idea that the worldling's "reality" is illusion and that life itself is a dream from which we shall eventually awake is of course a Buddhist one; but in Xueqin's hands it becomes a poetical means of demonstrating that his characters are both creatures of his imagination and at the same time the real companions of his golden youth. To that extent it can be thought of as a literary device rather than as a deeply held philosophy, though it is really both' (David Hawkes [trans.], *The Story of the Stone: A Chinese novel by Cao Xueqin, in Five Volumes* [Harmondsworth, Mddx, 1973], p. 45). The nearest that Cao Xueqin will get to the inwardness of Shen Zhou's meditation is his descriptions of flute-playing at night, vol. 3 chap. 76 (Penguin ed., pp. 507-526); compare also Andrew Plaks, *Archetype and Allegory in "Dream of the Red Chamber"* (Princeton, N.J., 1976), pp. 109-10, as cit. in Saussy, p. 29.

WRITTEN ON A FROSTY NIGHT

'Tis calm indeed! so calm, that it disturbs
And vexes meditation with its strange
And extreme silentness.
Samuel Taylor Coleridge

Like pushing aside layers and layers of reed stalks, at summer's end
when the aroma of firewood through chimneys wafts gently in the air
comes to me, creeping low, on a soft breeze–a calling
unfolds delicately, yet seems just around my eyelids,
when the color duckweed, swaying in clumps, stirs up bits of memory
when the long-tailed dragonfly flies toward me, hesitant,
and trembling, it hovers above the twilight-dyed ripples
and tries to land on a thorny water plant,
scattering powdery pistils, making dusk return to the swiftly
changing moment when I push aside layers and layers of reed stalks,
like pushing aside layers and layers of reed stalks at the end of that
faraway summer
So I see, like the last ashes in an incense burner
in front of the already dim altar that insists on shouting
in silence, trying hard to elevate the instant to an eternal memory
in my faint unease like transparent moth wings flapping
outside the window, sound of dried, broad leaves like hearts, blowing
about one by one,
circling in the wind before falling at random into the cool shade of the
empty courtyard,
I see an expanse of light on the startled pond at summer's end
lingering at ease, softly chanting a long, ancient tune, intending to
turn fate into luck when frogs croak at intervals in the lonely hour
when crickets besiege childhood wilderness, when I push aside layers and
layers of reed
stalks to find time slowly transcending summer's end

YANG MU (born Yang Ching-hsien, Taiwan, 1940), trans. from 'Shuangye Zuo' of 1985, in *No Trace of the Gardener; Poems of Yang Mu*, trans. Lawrence R. Smith and Michelle Yeh (New Haven, Conn., 1998), p. 192; see also Michelle Yeh, *Modern Chinese Poetry: Theory and Practice since 1917* (New haven, Conn., 1991), pp. 109-12, for slightly differing translation and also full discussion. The epigraph is the author's own placement, in English in the original.

J. H. Prynne, Gonville and Caius College, Cambridge,
revised October 2009

THE RHETORIC OF COMMENTARY

Carsten Madsen

Since Antiquity, and through history, commentary and rhetoric seem to have had a complicated relationship. They are both discursive practices, but appear to have been thought of as based on very different approaches to the textual and rhetorical situations in which they take place. Commentary, taken as an exegetic and strictly logical activity, forms its statements on the basis of analytic arguments and rhetoric develops its arguments in the form of enthymemes. Consequently, the art of making commentaries is perceived as being based on a scientific method using deductive reasoning and functioning on the epistemic basis of formal logic. Rhetoric (which Aristotle calls "the antistrophe of dialectic") seems to function primarily on the basis of informal logic and to deal with probability rather than scientific certainty. Nevertheless, in various historic formations of knowledge and language, commentary and rhetoric have deeply influenced one another, but often in such a discrete or implicit manner that it has been difficult to appreciate the relationship between the two. Particularly in the Middle Ages, the ancient distribution of commentary and rhetoric seems to have shifted in this direction towards two different epistemological grounds in a definitive way that still exerts an influence on the contemporary understanding of these discursive practices. As a result, it has been increasingly difficult to assess the relation between the two practices. Whereas commentary and rhetoric in Antiquity were assigned very precise functions in the ancient complex of textual, pedagogical, juridical, and political practices, these same functions undergo fundamental and somewhat obscure changes when systematized within the medieval *trivium.*

In the formation of *trivium* one can measure the extent to which these changes in the distribution of knowledge, skills, and competences within the realm of the verbal and logical arts took place between Antiquity and the Middle Ages. In the *trivium,* Aristotle's differentiated understanding of analytical, dialectical, and rhetorical argumentation is placed within a more constrained frame which does not allow for the same degree of differentiation. What we have thought of as "Aristotelian logic" since medieval times, Aristotle himself terms "analytics," whereas he reserves the term "logic" for "dialectics." Moreover, later references to the medieval *trivium* often substitute the word "logic" for "dialectic." But our concern here is more directed towards the difficulties of placing commentary, which in Antiquity was a well-defined verbal and logical art in its own right, within the *trivium.* Curiously, it is the Late Antique Latin commentator's extensive references to and appropriation of certain texts from Antiquity that facilitates the formation of *trivium*, but does the practice of commentary itself function under the auspice of grammar, dialectic, or rhetoric? And furthermore, how can we re-inscribe the ancient relationship between commentary and rhetoric in contemporary society for the benefit of today's textual and rhetorical practices?

In broad terms, I propose to describe commentary as a particular discursive form *within* the practice of rhetoric, a place to which it has never been formally ascribed. And more specifically, it is my contention that the future commentary should be construed in such a way that it would function within the rhetorical tradition that holds rhetoric to be epistemic in nature. This tradition goes back to what is known as the "Sophistic movement" of rhetoric, and in modern times it has been renewed in a seminal article from 1968 by Robert L. Scott called "On Viewing Rhetoric as Epistemic." What I am suggesting here opens a new area of investigation and therefore it is put forward in a more argumentative than demonstrative manner. Firstly, I will argue that there is a fundamental rhetoricity to commentary, not because of the linguistic nature of commentaries, though this certainly is an element of this topic worth discussion, but because of the very gesture of commentary on a prior text that has traditionally been presented by commentary as primary in relation to itself, so that commentary inscribes itself in the margin of the text, deemed to be of a secondary order. Secondly, I will suggest a historical and textual explanation as to why and how the genre of exegetical commentary has come to have a firm grasp on our understanding of commentary in general, an understanding that we are only beginning to break away from. And finally, we will briefly turn our attention to a few observations concerning the epistemological status of the rhetoric of commentary before and now.

First we have to establish an important principle concerning commentary. This practice is not only a question of annotating or glossing a text with explicatory commentaries; it does not only take place as a textual exegesis, although historically this seems to have been the most common model for understanding the practice of commentary. Ultimately, I am thinking of the full scope of the art of making commentaries, be it on texts, discourses, ideas, events, policies, conversations, people, things, or other commentaries. For practical reasons, however, I shall only refer to this relation as one between commentary and text. Of course, when referring to the genre of commentary today, the general public is probably prone to associating its discursive form with the sort of political criticism that we also call "political commentaries" or "political discussion," but I am aiming at commentary in its generality. In the rich historical archive of commentaries I will argue that it is possible to uncover a fundamental rhetoricity of commentary. Over the course of time such a trans-historical rhetoricity of commentary appears to have become increasingly clear. But what does this mean, "a fundamental rhetoricity of commentary"?

If we carefully examine the basic situation of making explicatory commentaries or annotations to a text–but indeed the use of any form of commentary–it seems reasonable to argue that there is something fundamentally rhetorical taking place. With his or her annotating gesture, the commentator is trying to sway the reader, or to be more precise, to *persuade* the reader to read an allegedly correct meaning into the text or a hidden truth out of the text. With this hermeneutic gesture the commentator is practicing an art very similar to that of a rhetorician: both are making use of *persuasio* in order to influence or appeal to an audience and to steer it towards the true meaning of the text or event in question. In both cases persuasion is used as a sort of demonstration; we are most fully persuaded about the correct meaning of a text, or the just and right course of action, or the appropriate sentiment in a situation when we consider a thing to have been demonstrated. But whereas the rhetorician has three modes of persuasion to appeal to his or her audience, it seems fair to say that the commentator traditionally has only made use of one or two. The rhetorician, as described in Aristotle's *On Rhetoric,* can appeal to the audience by using ethos, pathos, and logos.

> [There is persuasion] through character [*ethos*] whenever the speech is spoken in such a way as to make the speaker worthy of credence. . . . [There is persuasion] through the hearers when they are led to feel emotion [*pathos*] by the speech. . . . Persuasion occurs through the arguments [*logoi*]

> when we show the truth or the apparent truth from whatever is persuasive in each case. (Aristotle, pp. 38-39).

However, all these three modes of appeal are also at work in the art of commentary. We only believe a commentator's exegesis of a text when we find him or her credible. If we discover that we cannot trust a commentator, which is often the case–e.g., if something is added to or removed from the primary text–then we have a hermeneutic and interpretative problem, but we also have a rhetorical situation on our hands, since we are not convinced or persuaded by the commentator. Of course, the commentary may also stir the reader's feelings in many ways, so the persuasion about the true meaning of the text comes through the reader, but this mode of appeal is completely secondary to the commentary's appeal to logos. Through inferences, the commentator reasons what must be the correct exegesis of a text, and the reader is more likely persuaded to concur with an established truth of the text when the commentator is making argumentative claims about the full meaning of it based on logic.

So the situation of making commentaries on a text can easily, and more fully, be described as a rhetorical situation which gives us an elaborate conceptual framework for understanding what is going on in this discursive practice. The rhetoric of commentary and its fundamental rhetoricity become even more understandable within the principles used in contemporary rhetorical criticism. Very similar to rhetorical criticism, commentary defines, classifies, analyzes, interprets and evaluates a text, but in this context we shall limit ourselves to considering classical rhetoric.

Now, this general approach to the practice of commentary may seem speculative, were it not based on some empirical observations, so we will turn our attention to the historical development of commentary and rhetoric in the transition of the rhetorical education and pedagogical practices from Antiquity to the Middle Ages. In most schools of the Hellenistic and Roman period and all the way up towards the end of Antiquity, the scholarly tradition is focused on exegetical and scholastic practices. From the beginning, these different practices, most notably perhaps that of philosophy in Greece, are intimately linked to life and work in private and public schools. One of the most important activities in philosophical schools was directed towards the explication of the texts of the school's founder. In his article, "What was Commentary in Late Antiquity? The Example of the Neoplatonic Commentators," Philippe Hoffman explains:

> The practice of exegesis of written texts supplanted the ancient practice of dialogue. It was sustained through its application to canonical texts, and was put to everyday use in the framework of courses in the explication of texts. The social reality of the school as an institution–with its hierarchy, its successor to the school's founder, its buildings for religious assembly and worship in which communal life was practiced, its library, its regulation of time, and its programs organized around the reading of canonical texts–constitutes a concrete context into which we should reinsert the practice of commentary, the exegesis, which is the heart of philosophical pedagogy and the matrix of doctrinal and dogmatic works. (Hoffman, p. 597)

Now, it is difficult to pinpoint when classical civilization ends and the Middle Ages begin, and perhaps even more difficult to say when the history of classical rhetoric ends. But there is not much doubt that the scholarly tradition at the end of Antiquity came to serve as the model for medieval rhetoric and for the practice of making exegetical commentaries on canonical rhetorical texts in order to rebuild the intellectual life of the Middle Ages. To a large extent, the exegetical commentaries on mostly Ciceronian rhetoric can be taken as key texts in the formation of medieval rhetoric and, indeed, the formation of the medieval scholarly tradition and medieval theology. The survival of Ciceronian rhetoric into the Middle Ages is mainly due to the Late Antique Latin commentators, but during this transformation, when the *trivium* is being formed, the focus of rhetoric shifts as the doctrine of classical rhetoric becomes more closely associated with dialectic and less with the practical art of oratory. In this process, rhetoric becomes intellectualized and develops into a more textually oriented and pedagogical practice than was the case at Cicero's time. Oratory, which in the Roman Empire owes so much to Cicero's practice and definition, had declined steadily under political conditions that in the long run could not uphold the strong oratorical traditions of earlier periods, most significantly those of forensic and deliberative oratory. The *Encyclopedia of Rhetoric* stresses how this transformation is due to a growing attention to intellectual and logical aspects of rhetoric that could serve ecclesiastical interests: "rhetorical teaching survived through late Antiquity and into the Middle Ages because of its intellectual and cultural prestige. And in the course of this appropriation it came to take on new forms and find new purposes among which, of course, the ecclesiastical forms and purposes came to dominate" (Copeland and Ziokowski, p. 487, 837).

Here we have a very complicated historical development. In the Middle Ages rhetoric is revived, that is, mainly Ciceronian rhetoric, whereas the majority of Greek rhetoric had to wait till the Renaissance to be rediscovered. But in order to recapture and transform the art of rhetoric, both medieval rhetoric and Renaissance rhetoric had to rely heavily on exegetical commentaries. In the process of glossing, annotating, translating, and in other textual ways appropriating early Ciceronian rhetoric, certain parts of the rhetoric were preferred over others–namely, those very parts that would affirm the textual practices of the ecclesiastical discursive forms and of the exegetical commentary itself. These parts all had a close relation to the art of dialectic, which can be taken as an indication of a dominating preference for appeals to *logos* and to inferential logic. So what is being constructed in medieval rhetoric and in the practice of exegetical commentary is a complex connection uniting dialectic logic, theology, exegesis, commentary, and the "revelation" of a fixed truth already contained in canonical texts, needing only to be made explicit.

The historical evidence for this preference is overwhelming, but we cannot go into great detail on this matter. It is significant, however, that it is mainly Cicero's early treatise *De inventione* that came to be the authority on rhetoric by the fourth century, whereas neither Cicero's far more fully developed work, *De Oratore,* nor Quintilian's *Institutio Oratoria* came to play any major role, even though these works were still easily available at the time. In *A New History of Classical Rhetoric,* in a chapter on "The Survival of Classical Rhetoric from Late Antiquity to the Middle Ages," George Kennedy explains:

> The reason is not difficult to grasp. *On Invention* combined Ciceronian authority with the kind of succinct, dry exposition of theory that could be reduced to lists and be memorized. Students, and most teachers as well, were not interested in, and probably often not capable of understanding, longer and more complex discussions of rhetoric. (Kennedy, p. 276)

Still, it is remarkable that it was Cicero's early, more schematic and even incomplete treatise that came to be the shaping influence on medieval rhetorical teaching. This in itself tells us much about the interests and institutional character of medieval rhetoric and commentary.

However, seen from a strictly rhetorical perspective, the particular use of exegetical commentaries in the Middle Ages, with its strong appeal to *logos,* in fact marks the beginning of a long historical decline of rhetoric that even the rich Renaissance rhetoric could not prevent. Rhetoric was studied continuously as an essential element of the *trivium*, one of the *artes sermocinales* or arts of language, along with grammar and dialectic, but in medieval rhetoric and commentary, it appears that grammar and dialectic have been the main structuring factors. If we consider a few elements of the appropriation of rhetoric in the Middle Ages, it becomes quite clear how the parts of the ancient rhetorical tradition that are most easily associated with dialectics are favored. Copeland and Ziolkowski carefully mark out some of the important events in this history:

> Isidore, Bishop of Seville (seventh century) devotes a book of his encyclopedia of knowledge, the *Etymologiae*, to rhetoric (basing his treatment on Cicero and Late Antique summaries of Ciceronian texts); Alcuin (eighth century) records his efforts to teach the art of rhetoric to Charlemagne; and from the early Middle Ages onward, a clearly Ciceronian rhetorical theory is routinely featured in the curricula of monasteries in northern and southern Europe. The monasteries also contributed a great deal to the conservation and transmission of rhetorical texts. There is an unbroken tradition of academic commentary on the *On Invention* (called the 'old rhetoric,' *rhetorica vetus*), culminating in the work of the twelfth-century cathedral schools in France and Germany, where rhetoric was studied as a close partner of dialectic, and where *On Invention* was read alongside Cicero's *Topics* and other related texts on dialectical topics. Commentaries on the *Ad Herennium* (*rhetorica nova*) also begin to appear in the eleventh and twelfth centuries in these northern European schools, with new attention directed to the stylistic teaching in Book 4. (Copeland and Ziolkowski, p. 488, 837)

Also, in the arts faculties in Paris and Oxford, logic was the dominant subject, and rhetoric seems to have assumed the role that it had taken in the earlier cathedral schools, as another dimension of dialectical study. For convenience, I take the liberty of citing further from Copeland and Ziolkowski's excellent survey of this history in *Encyclopedia of Rhetoric:*

> Aristotle's *On Rhetoric* was translated into Latin from Greek by William Moerbeke about 1270 (a translation and commentary based on an Arabic version of Aristotle's text had circulated earlier). The new Latin translation of the *On Rhetoric* seems to have had an immediate impact at Paris, where it was commented on by several masters between the late thirteenth and the mid-fourteenth centuries, and where copies of the text itself were distributed by the university stationers. But Aristotle's text found no official place in a university curriculum until the 1431 Oxford statutes, where it is mentioned along with Boethius's *De topicis differentiis* Book 4 and the *Ad Herennium:* these statues may reflect teaching practices that were ongoing and long established by the fifteenth century. If indeed Aristotle's *On Rhetoric* was being taught at Oxford and Paris, it would likely have been read in relation to the texts of Aristotle's *Organon* (the logic texts of the Aristotelian canon), which, by the late thirteenth century, formed the backbone of the curriculum in the arts faculties. Aristotle's definition of rhetoric as the 'antistrophe' of dialectic, an art of discourse that draws its techniques from the same pool as dialectic, offered a newfound theoretical justification for what had been the actual institutional place of rhetoric as a counterpart of dialectical study in the urban schools of the twelfth and thirteenth centuries . . . Augustine's treatise *De doctrina christiana* deserves to be considered the first Christian rhetoric. This text sets into motion a theological tradition of rhetoric which takes the form not only of preaching, but of scriptural interpretation, semiotics (theory of signs and symbols within and beyond language), and spiritual disciplines of reading and meditation. Before his conversion, Augustine had been a professional rhetorician, both as teacher and orator. But in *De doctrina christiana* (written between 396 and 427 ce), Augustine explicitly reacts against the classical (Ciceronian) rhetorical inheritance. . . . Augustine treats discovery (invention) in terms of techniques of scriptural exegesis: these include philology and grammar; a knowledge of the difference between literal and figurative language;

> and most importantly, a semiotic theory (grounded in philosophical and theological principles) that distinguishes between signs (words and other symbols) and things (truths and realities, especially spiritual realities) to which signs must refer. It is in laying down this semiotic theory, the distinction between linguistic signs and truths, that Augustine reintroduces, now in Christian theological terms, the old Platonic distrust of rhetoric as manipulation of language detached from truth. In the Augustinian model of rhetoric, invention is a process of interpreting a text, the Bible, in which all truths have already been revealed. The notion that truth is fixed, that the subject matter (the truth of salvation) has already been revealed, and that this subject matter will always be the same in any Christian discourse, underwrites Augustine's theory of delivery, the 'means of setting forth that which has been understood. . . . Augustine had captured the textual and textually interpretive character of Late Antique Jewish and Christian culture, and had articulated this exegetical imperative in rhetorical terms: invention, the key intellectual process of rhetoric, was converted to the discovery and hermeneutical penetration of truths contained in writing. One could argue that if the master genre of Roman antiquity was the forensic oration, the master genre of medieval culture was exegesis. (*ibid.,* 489-91, 837)

In this historical process of appropriating the ancient art of rhetoric by way of glossing, annotating, translating, and so forth, medieval rhetoric develops as a series of commentaries on the early Cicero, commentaries that function in their own right, but by no means form an actual continuation of the rhetorical tradition from Antiquity. Interestingly, it is this historical transformation that delineates two very different approaches to rhetoric and commentary, two approaches that belong to two epistemological realms that differ in nature and do not share the same fundamental understanding concerning language and thinking–for example, of what it means to speak and listen, to write and read, and to think and understand. What is the reason for this transformation of the two verbal arts that appear to have been functioning on more equal terms in Antiquity? In answering this question we have to appreciate the striking difference between the ways that Antiquity was inherited in the Middle Ages and during the beginning of modernity. Condemning *originality* and showing a faithful respect for the ancients was an intellectual virtue in the Middle Ages, and the scholarly tradition openly regarded itself as a mere unfolding of doctrines contained in the ancient texts from which emanated *authority*. The commentator presented himself as merely an exegete of old doctrines, despite the fact, in this case, that he drastically altered the whole teaching of rhetoric. So even though medieval commentators thought of themselves as faithful to the rhetoric and the tradition of commentary from Antiquity, they did in fact construe the relationship between these two verbal arts very differently by making use of commentary as the logical conveyance and appropriation of rhetoric. Philippe Hoffmann comments on this way of appropriating ancient doctrines:

> A foundational study by P. Hadot (1968) has revealed the philosophical fecundity of misunderstandings or incomprehensions of the meaning of texts: they are the ancient and medieval way of producing 'doctrines.' Since philosophizing consisted essentially in conducting the exegesis of 'Authorities,' the search for truth was most frequently confounded with the search for the meaning of texts held to be authoritative on essential philosophical and theological questions, the truth already contained in these texts needing only to be made explicit. Hence, as the majority of philosophical and theological problems were posed in exegetical terms, theoretical developments proceeded according to a method we may describe as: (1) arbitrarily systematizing disparate formulations extracted from completely unrelated contexts; (2) amalgamating likewise disparate philosophical notions or concepts originating in different or even contradictory doctrines; and (3) explicating notions not to be found at all in the original. (Hoffmann, p. 602)

During the beginning of modernity, a new image of the commentator arises; the truth is no longer to be found in the ancient texts but rather in the commentary itself. Now the commentator himself becomes the *authority* on the textual tradition on which he makes his commentaries. The exegete still restores and comments upon the ancient texts according to strictly logical principles such as those of philology, but he also makes this textual tradition available to original interpretations. A prime example is Nietzsche, who ultimately turns against philology in order to reinvent Antiquity on contemporary terms. In Nietzsche's view, the classical scholar, the medieval exegete, is a hindrance to the development of the potentialities of ancient culture, and in *We Philologists* he goes on to say: "The classicist of the future as skeptic of our entire culture, and thereby destroyer of professional philology. . . . *Task for philology:* disappearance" (Nietzsche 1988, p. 56 and p. 77).

So what can we conclude from the medieval appropriation of the ancient scholarly tradition under these textual conditions with its strong emphasis on analytic logic? I have suggested how the epistemological foundation of the medieval exegetical commentary came to dominate the art of commentary, as well as that of rhetoric, for a very long time, with a few exceptions–such as Nietzsche. Furthermore, it is my contention that we are only beginning to glimpse the possibility of a new rhetoric of commentary that breaks away from the firm grasp that analytic logic has had on it since the Middle Ages. The task at hand today is to find a new epistemological foundation for commentary that takes into consideration the fundamental rhetoricity of commentary we initially touched upon. One possibility is to adapt Robert L. Scott's view in his article "On Viewing Rhetoric as Epistemic," in which he backs away from the Aristotelian notion of truth and analytic arguments as a starting point for rhetoric. "The attractiveness," he says, "of the analytic ideal, ordinarily only dimly grasped but nonetheless powerfully active in the rhetoric of those who deem truth as prior and enabling, lies in the smuggling of the sense of certainty into human affairs" (Scott, p. 312). Instead he turns towards the sophists, who were ignored in the Middle Ages: "The sophists facing their experiences found consistently not *logos* . . . but *dissoi logoi,* that is contradictory claims" (*ibid.,* p. 315). But this is also the case when we think about commentary, also the medieval exegetical commentary. Commentaries make *claims* about how to read a text, they argue a truth, but the truth is not prior to commentary or hidden in the text. Quite the contrary, there is always the possibility of other commentaries making contradictory claims which the commentators have to take into account when arguing their cases. But, as we can conclude, commentary is not secondary to a primary text, commentary *creates* the truth, and in this sense commentary is epistemic, it creates knowledge.

WORKS CITED

Aristotle: *On Rhetoric. A Theory of Civic Discourse,* translated by George A. Kennedy, 2nd ed. (New York and Oxford: Oxford University Press 2007)

Rita Copeland and Jan Ziolkowski: "Medieval Rhetoric", in *Encyclopedia of Rhetoric,* ed. Thomas O. Sloane (Oxford: Oxford University Press 2006).

Pierre Hadot: "Philosophie, exégèse et contre-sens," in *Akten des XIV. internationalen Kongresses für Philosophie,* vol. 1, 1968, pp. 333-39. Reprinted in P. Hadot: *Études de Philosophie Ancienne,* pp. 3-11 (Paris: Les Belles Lettres 1998).

Philippe Hoffmann: *A Companion to Ancient Philosophy,* Edited by: Mary Louise Gill and Pierre Pellegrin 2009 Blackwell Publishing Ltd. Maiden and Oxford

George A. Kennedy: *A New History of Classical Rhetoric* (Princeton University Press: Princeton 1994)

Friedrich Nietzsche: *Wir Philologen,* in *Kritische Studienausgabe,* vol. 8, eds. G. Colli and M. Montinari (München, Berlin and New York, 1988)

Robert L. Scott: "On Viewing Rhetoric as Epistemic", in *Professing the New Rhetorics: A Sourcebook,* eds. T. Enos and S.C. Brown (Allyn & Bacon 1994)

Carsten Madsen is Associate Professor at the Center for Rhetoric, Department of Aesthetic Studies, Aarhus University, Denmark. He has written books and articles on poetry, aesthetics, philosophy, and architectural theory, and is currently doing research on 1) the rhetorical relationship between language, knowledge, and probability in Sophism and in Nietzsche's work on rhetoric; 2) the uses of commentary from antiquity to the present day, particularly in contemporary politics; and 3) Talkaoke as a rhetorical model for public debate.

FOURTY-FOUR WAYS OF LOOKING AT MARGINALIA

Louis Bury

Louis Bury teaches literature at NYU and is an English Ph.D. candidate at the CUNY Graduate Center, where he is at work on a constraint-based dissertation about constraint-based writing.

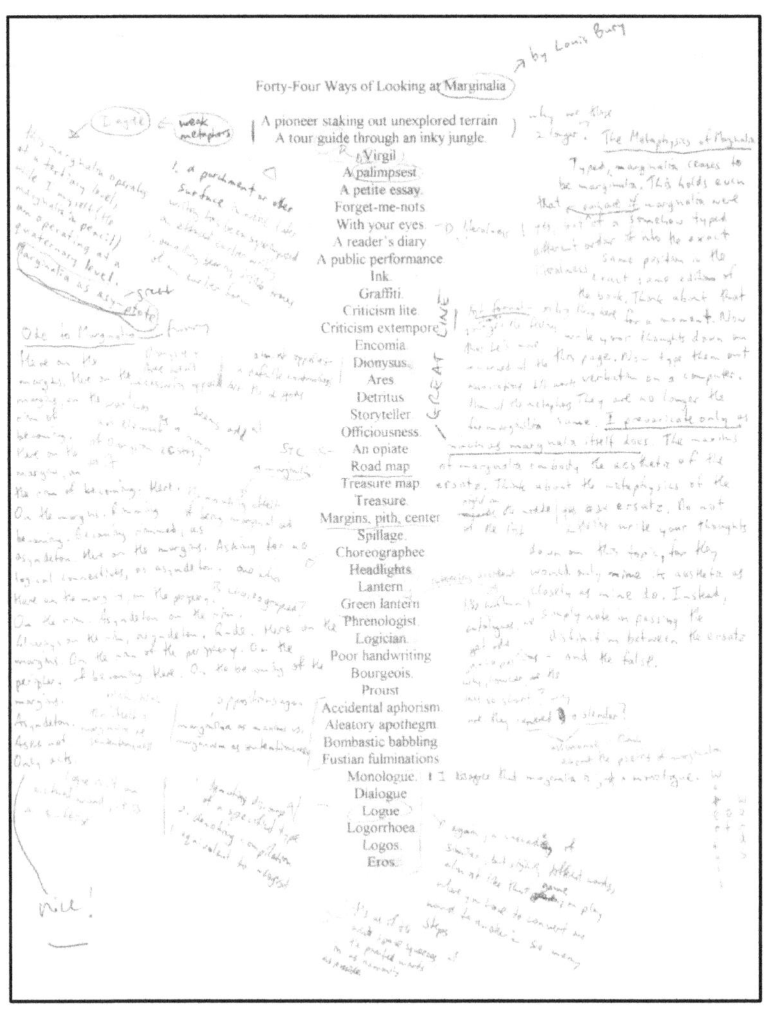

Forty-Four Ways of Looking at Marginalia

A pioneer staking out unexplored terrain
A tour guide through an inky jungle
Virgil
A palimpsest
A petite essay
Forget-me-nots
With your eyes
A reader's diary
A public performance
Ink
Graffiti
Criticism lite
Criticism extempore
Encomia
Dionysus
Ares
Detritus
Storyteller
Officiousness
An opiate
Road map
Treasure map
Treasure
Margins, pith, center
Spillage
Choreographee
Headlights
Lantern
Green lantern
Phrenologist
Logician
Poor handwriting
Bourgeois
Proust
Accidental aphorism
Aleatory apothegm
Bombastic babbling
Fustian fulminations
Monologue
Dialogue
Logue
Logorrhoea
Logos
Eros

[See http://glossator.org for original image]

A CURIOUS MISTAKE CONCERNING CRANIAL SUTURES IN ARISTOTLE'S *PARTS OF ANIMALS*, OR, THE USE AND ABUSE OF THE FOOTNOTE

Barbara Clayton

> It is difficult to speak of Aristotle without exaggeration: he is felt to be so mighty, and is known to be so wrong. (George Henry Lewes, *Aristotle: A Chapter from the History of Science*)[1]

Aristotle's biological writings have elicited high praise from those who study his work. For although from a scientific point of view they may have been rendered obsolete long ago, it is in these texts that some of Aristotle's most impressive qualities as a researcher and a thinker are to be found: his collection of massive amounts of data and the organization of all this material into a coherent whole. As Jonathan Barnes writes in *Aristotle, A Very Short Introduction*, "It is easy to become starry-eyed over the *Researches*, which are on any account a work of genius and a monument of indefatigable industry."[2] Naturally Aristotle, inasmuch as he had few tools other than patience and what must have been incredibly good eyesight, made a few mistakes. Some of these–such as his description of the European bison's ability to expel its feces to a distance of 24 feet, or his claim that male humans (as well as male sheep, goats and pigs) have more teeth than their female counterparts–have become notorious.[3] However, in some respects it is these very mistakes, and not Aristotle's biological observations themselves that are of interest

[1] Lewes 1864, 1.

[2] Barnes 2000, 20.

[3] As Bertrand Russell noted, "Aristotle could have avoided the mistake of thinking that women have fewer teeth than men, by the simple device of asking Mrs. Aristotle to keep her mouth open while he counted," (Russell 1950, 103). Bison example quoted by Barnes, ibid.

to the modern scholar. Why were they made? What concatenation of events or erroneous assumptions might have caused Aristotle to make these false assertions? In the case of the European bison, it may have simply been that, in Barnes' words, "Aristotle was taken in by a tipsy huntsman's after-dinner yarn." But in the case of the dental inferiority of females in some species we might wonder whether Aristotle was led astray by the prevailing gender bias of his time. This, in fact, is what Robert Mayhew decided to explore in his 2004 study, *The Female in Aristotle's Biology*. Mayhew reviews a series of mistakes in Aristotle's biological writings all having to do with gender difference. Mayhew's objective was to determine whether these mistakes were the result of certain ideological presuppositions about males and females common to the ancient Greeks of Aristotle's day, or simply bad science. He concludes that Aristotle's mistakes were not dictated by cultural misogyny.

It is not my purpose here to assess whether or not Mayhew succeeds. Instead I would like to focus on one particular Aristotelian mistake he discusses, an erroneous claim concerning a different pattern of cranial sutures in men and women.[4] Mayhew's solution to this error was first proposed in 1882 by the translator and commentator William Ogle. However, since Mayhew is constructing an argument–namely that Aristotle is not influenced by gender bias in the case of cranial sutures–in addition to presenting Ogle's proposed solution he footnotes other scholars who have examined this Aristotelian mistake. In other words, Mayhew is relying here upon two different forms of scholarship: the commentary and the footnote. Consequently, Mayhew's discussion of the cranial sutures mistake affords an opportunity to think about how footnotes operate differently than commentary, both in terms of narrative voice and narrative desire.

The commentator's voice is her own and no other; it is univocal. Commentary offers an explanatory narrative, a possible

[4] The cranial sutures mistake is a frequently cited example of Aristotle's fallibility, and often mentioned in conjunction with his mistake about gender difference and teeth. I suspect the reason is that both mistakes could presumably have been rectified with more careful observation, and thus they leave Aristotle especially open to the charge of cultural bias. In his 1955 study of Aristotle Louis Bourgey chooses the cranial sutures mistake, which he qualifies as one of Aristotle's "famous errors," to represent the entire family of mistakes behind criticism of Aristotle's lack of independence from ideology. Bourgey 1955, 84.

resolution of a problematic passage representing the desire to fix an aberration or to correct a mistake. And yet any explanation can be seen as an invitation (or demand) for further exploration and thus contains its own potential open-endedness and plurality. Writing about the classical commentary, Christina Kraus describes how the process of explaining produces "a kind of meta-narrative" with the ability to generate further narratives endlessly:

> On a more (ludic) theoretical level, the give and take between the text and its commentary, and between the commentary and its reader, is a complex manifestation of the pull of narrative desire: a commentary becomes a kind of meta-narrative, a story told about, and around, a text based on the tension between the disorder created by a problematic, or multiply-meaning, source-text, and the order generated by the satisfaction of the text's teasing answered–or only deferred?–by the commentator's judgment; and in a kind of *mise en abyme*, on the tension between the meaning fixed by the commentator's "answer" and the plurality of meaning(s) inevitably opened by the new paths suggested by the very process of answering.[5]

By contrast, in the footnote, the individual voice disappears. Via a footnote, an author joins a scholarly community, adding the *auctoritas* of other scholars to her own. As Stevens and Williams observe: "The footnote is written by an individual whose own voice has been rendered into a collective voice of similarly educated authors. That is, in the footnote the individual author purposefully loses his or her writerly voice to become part of this collective."[6] In terms of narrative voice then, footnote and commentary are diametrically opposed.

At first glance, the same would seem to hold true for narrative desire. Commentary, as Kraus stated above, sets up a relationship between reader and text in which the desire to explain represents a singular answer that can theoretically never be permanently fixed in its singularity. Footnotes, on the other hand, inscribe the opposite trajectory when considered from the point of view of the author: the plurality of corroborating voices represents a desire to confirm a

[5] Kraus 2002, 9.
[6] Stevens and Williams 2006, 211.

singular position or argument, and thus confer the stability of consensus. Commentary is potentially destabilizing; footnotes, in principle, are not. However, in terms of the relationship between *reader* and text there is another, different kind of desire operating in the footnote, one I would qualify as metonymic. Footnotes are textual abbreviations, sometimes literally and always figuratively. Like icebergs, they show only the smallest part of their entirety. A footnote is an invitation to know more, to see a bigger picture. It is this metonymic desire that I would like to explore, using Mayhew's footnote in his explanation of the cranial sutures mistake.

Unlike Mayhew, I am not particularly interested in the scientific accuracy behind Aristotle's observation. In fact, for the most part we read Aristotle's biological writings today more for meaning–how Aristotle understood the natural world and the creatures who live in it–rather than for scientific truth. Yet meaning and truth are not mutually exclusive by any means; they are constantly informing one another. What we must confront critically is our desire for fixed meaning and certainty in our endeavors, and the various temptations to overlook irregularities that this desire throws our way. By unpacking Mayhew's note and restoring what has been occluded there I want to transform his resolution of a perplexing passage into a destabilizing multiplicity of narratives. In Latin, to make a mistake (*errare*) is also to wander. Mayhew's presentation of Aristotle's curious mistake concerning cranial sutures provides an occasion to wander through a maze of scholarship in which footnotes, if allowed to speak fully–and especially if they are allowed to speak to each other–have interesting stories of their own to tell.

THE MISTAKE

In Chapter 7 of the second book of *Parts of Animals* Aristotle says that among animals the human male brain is the largest with respect to his size, and that men's brains are larger than women's.[7] Here he is correct. The human brain is large for an animal of his size, and by and large the brains of men are slightly larger than those of women.[8]

---

[7] ἔχει δὲ τῶν ζῴων ἐγκέφαλον πλεῖστον ἄνθρωπος ὡς κατὰ μέγεθος, καὶ τῶν ἀνθρώπων οἱ ἄρρενες τῶν θηλειῶν (653a27). (Of animals the human has the biggest brain in accordance with size, and of humans males [bigger than] females.)

[8] Passingham 2008, 33: "The human brain is 3.5 times bigger than expected for an ape our size." Blum (referenced by Mayhew) 1997, 37: "There is an

Aristotle goes on to say that men have more sutures in their skulls than women, and that the reason for this is that the sutures supply a place for the brain to receive air (to cool it down), and bigger brains (being hotter) require more sutures.[9] While this makes a great deal of sense from an Aristotelian point of view, he is wrong. Anatomically speaking, the skulls of men and women are identical; they have the same number of sutures.[10]

Two passages from Aristotle's *History of Animals* (1.7 and 3.7) offer additional details, and explain precisely what Aristotle meant when he said that there were more sutures in male skulls than in female skulls. In these passages he claims that the skulls of women have one circular suture, whereas the skulls of men have three, which come together in the shape of a triangle.[11] As we now know, the number of sutures in the adult human skull, not counting the bones of the face, is sixteen.[12] However, the most prominent are three in number: the coronal, which runs across the top of the forehead more or less from temple to temple; the sagittal, which bisects the coronal; and the lambdoid, which looks like the Greek letter *lambda* (Λ) at the

overall size difference [in the brains of men and women]: by weighing and measuring hundreds of human brains, researchers have found that, in general, men's brains are about 15 percent larger than women's brains."

9 καὶ ῥαφὰς δὲ πλείστας ἔχει περὶ τὴν κεφαλήν, καὶ τὸ ἄρρεν πλείους τῶν θηλειῶν, διὰ τὴν αὐτὴν αἰτίαν, ὅπως ὁ τόπος εὔπνους ᾖ, καὶ μᾶλλον ὁ πλείων ἐγκέφαλος (653b1-3). (And [a human] has more sutures around the skull, and the male more than females, on account of the same reason [i.e., the bigger size], in order that the place may have breath in it [in other words, be ventilated], and the more [breath] the larger the brain.)

10 In fact, Aristotle may be wrong on both counts. According to Blum, research using PET scanning–positron emission tomography, a type of nuclear medicine used to create images of what is inside the body–suggests that the brains of woman are actually slightly hotter than those of men. (Blum 1997, 53.)

11 Book 1.7: ἔχει δὲ ῥαφὰς τῶν μὲν γυναικῶν μίαν κύκλῳ, τῶν δ' ἀνδρῶν τρεῖς εἰς ἓν συναπτούσας ὡς ἐπὶ τὸ πολύ (491b3-5). ([The skulls] of women have sutures that are one, in a circle; [the skulls] of men have sutures that are three, touching together at one [spot], for the most part.) Book 3.7: καὶ τούτου τὸ μὲν θῆλυ κύκλῳ ἔχει τὴν ῥαφήν, τὸ δ'ἄρρεν τρεῖς ῥαφὰς ἄνωθεν συναπτούσας, τριγωνοειδεῖς (516a18-20). (And of this [the skull] the female has a suture in a circle, while the male has three sutures touching together above, triangular in form.

12 *Dorland's Illustrated Medical Dictionary*, 2000, pp. 1738-9. Interestingly, this number may vary slightly depending upon which reference one consults.

back of the skull. Where the sagittal suture meets the lambdoid we see an upside down "Y" shape, or what appear to be *three* sutures–Aristotle would have considered the lambdoid suture to be two separate sutures–meeting at a triangular point, just as Aristotle described in the case of the male skull.

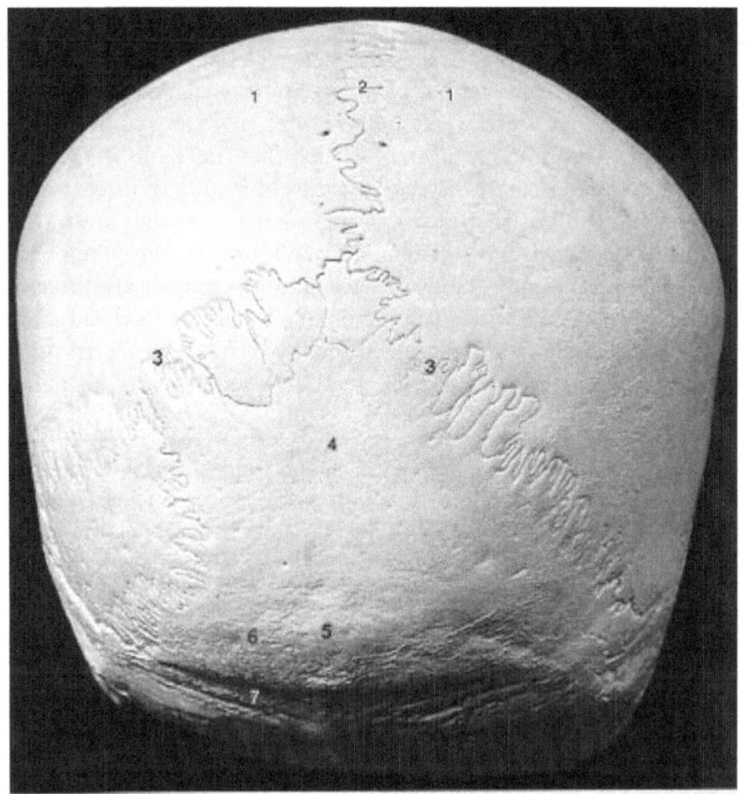

(Posterior view of the skull showing the sagittal and lambdoid sutures. Photo courtesy of Dr. James A. Strauss, Pennsylvania State University, Biology 29, *Human Anatomy*.) Note that Aristotle's total number of sutures does not include the coronal suture.

THE SOLUTION

Mayhew turns to William Ogle, the 19th century translator and commentator of *Parts of Animals*, for a possible reason behind Aristotle's claim for different numbers of sutures in the skulls of men and women. He writes, "William Ogle provides an explanation for how Aristotle might have come to this erroneous conclusion while at the same time being committed to the importance of observation."[13] Mayhew then goes on to quote a section from Ogle's note on this passage:

> Of course the opportunities of seeing a female skull would be much fewer than of seeing a male skull; for battle-fields would no longer be of service. Still it is not impossible that A.'s statement may have been founded on some single observation. For it is by no means uncommon for the sutures on the vertex to become more or less effaced in pregnant women; so common indeed is it, that the name "puerperal osteophyte" has been given to the condition by Rokitansky [here Mayhew omits Ogle's bibliographic reference, *Path. Anat.* Iii. 208, *Syd. Soc. Transl.*]. A woman's skull may have been observed in which the Sagittal suture had thus disappeared; when the Lamboid [*sic*; the mistake occurs in Mayhew's text, not Ogle's], with the lateral sutures, and the Coronal, might fairly be described as forming together a circular suture. It must not be forgotten what great difficulty there was in A.'s time in getting a sight of human bones. (1882, 168n26).

I will return to Ogle's proposed solution later. Here I note that Mayhew is primarily concerned with whether or not Aristotle actually saw a female skull that seemed to have only one suture. He does not question Ogle's hypothesis that if the skull came from a pregnant woman, chances are that it would have the pathological condition discovered by Rokitansky leading to the appearance of a singular, circular suture. Or, in Mayhew's own words:

> Following Ogle's lead, we can speculate that Aristotle perhaps had the opportunity to examine only a single female skull–or at any rate, not likely more than a couple–which came from a woman (or women) who died in childbirth or during a complicated pregnancy. He observed one suture in this skull (or these skulls) and so concluded

[13] Mayhew 2004, 73.

> that a man normally had three sutures, whereas a woman had only one.[14]

Recast in the language of our period, Ogle's solution sounds plausible. However, it still requires that Aristotle knew the skull came from a woman, that this woman died while pregnant, and that she had a pathological condition that would have changed the exterior of her skull. Given Greek attitudes towards burial and disposal of the dead, we must add to the various components of this speculation the question of provenance.[15] Where would such a skull have come from? A curiosity brought back from a foreign land? A grave accidently opened in which a woman dead in childbirth was known to have been buried? Clearly support is needed here, and Mayhew obliges with a footnote, which reads:

> Ogle's point is cited in Lloyd (1983, 102n165), and Dean-Jones (1994, 81); see Lennox (2001a. 211-12). D. W. Thompson writes: "I imagine that this singular misstatement dates from a belief that the sutures of the skull coincided with the margin and the partings of the hairy scalp" (1910, ad 491b4, n7).[16]

At this point it is worth pausing to consider the role of the footnote in scholarship that deals with texts like Aristotle's biological writings. Lloyd, Dean-Jones, Lennox and Mayhew himself are primarily classicists, not scientists. They must rely upon the scientific credentials and presumed accuracy of their 19th century predecessor William Ogle, who was a physician by training. They thus represent a unique intersection of author, text, and previous scholarship that follows neither the model of literary criticism, nor that of scientific texts. Von Staden addresses this point in an essay on Galen's commentators:

> One consequence of the disappearance of the commentary genre from twentieth-century scientists' and doctors'

[14] Ibid., 74.
[15] See Kurtz and Boardman 1971 who mention death in childbirth as meriting special treatment (331). It seems highly unlikely that the bones of a woman who died in childbirth would be readily available for observation.
[16] Mayhew, 74.

> arsenal has been that commentaries on ancient Greek medical and scientific texts have largely become the *chasse gardée* of classicists (sometimes with little or no visible expertise in science), of a handful of professional historians of science trained in the ancient languages (particularly in the case of the exact sciences), and of an occasional specialist in Greek poetry. . . . Unlike Hipparchus, Galen, Eutocius, and other ancient commentators, some of their more recent counterparts display little or no interest in the scientific validity of ancient observations, concepts, or theories, let alone in the efficacy of the scientific practices presented in the ancient texts on which they comment.[17]

Mayhew's references, G. E. R. Lloyd, Leslie Dean-Jones and James Lennox, are all significant and influential contributors to the field of Aristotelian studies and ancient science in the late 20th and early 21st centuries. (Thompson, also mentioned in Mayhew's footnote, is a closer contemporary of William Ogle than of these scholars, so he will be dealt with separately.) Mayhew needs to reinforce Ogle's proposition–that Aristotle's mistake came from a skull affected by the puerperal osteophyte condition–with as much scholarly authority as he can muster, but, given that most of his readers will be classicists, he has chosen classical scholars rather than scientists to supply it. He does not need to worry about the puerperal osteophyte theory *per se*, because, as his footnote suggests, neither Lloyd, Dean-Jones, nor Lennox was particularly worried about it. Mayhew is content to let William Ogle (and Ogle's cited reference, Karl Rokitansky) serve as a guarantee that in this instance a gender difference that might have seemed to support Aristotle's assumptions of female inferiority was simply a matter of fortuitous pathology. He does not consider the possibility that Ogle's scientific information might be flawed.

Let us return to William Ogle's original note in his commentary. Mayhew's quotation of Ogle's note ends with the sentence, "It must not be forgotten what great difficulty there was in A.'s time in getting a sight of human bones." Mayhew has chosen to omit the last part of Ogle's note, which continues as follows:

> Even much later Galen, it is said, went all the way to Egypt for the purpose of seeing merely a bronze representation of

[17] Von Staden 2002, 125-6.

> the human skeleton (*Cuvier, Hist. d. Sc.* i. 59). A well-known story is told of Democritus, how he was in the habit of wandering about among tombs and was therefore supposed by his fellow-citizens to be mad; and how the great Hippocrates was sent to see him, and, having heard his account, pronounced him not only to be sane, but the sanest of men. Cuvier explains this strange habit of Democritus, by supposing that his object was to find "quelques pieces ostéoligiques"![18]

Ogle has supplied two anecdotes–both taken from Cuvier's *magnum opus*, the posthumously published (1841) five volume, *Histoire des sciences naturelles, depuis leur origine jusqu'à nos jours chez tous les peuples connus professée au Collège de France* [History of the natural sciences among all known peoples from their beginning to the present day presented to the College of France]–to demonstrate the point that scientists in the ancient world had difficult access to human bones. Why would Mayhew leave out the end of Ogle's note? Surely because this kind of narrative seems out of place in his own argument. Again we are faced with the uneasy positioning of Mayhew's text somewhere in between the world of the scientist and the world of the classicist. Mayhew needs Ogle to sound like a scientist because Ogle is offering possible scientific proof that Aristotle saw a female skull that appeared to have only one circular suture. In the anecdotes about Galen and Democritus, however, the voice of Ogle as scientist modulates into Ogle as classicist and philologist, i.e., someone who is interested in language and narrative. Indeed, the story about Democritus is more complicated than it might at first seem to be. The main idea is that Democritus' desire for knowledge about the human body leads him to engage in behavior–wandering around graveyards–that was considered abnormal by his compatriots. Their concern brings a famous physician, Hippocrates, who vouches for the sanity of Democritus. In other words, this is a story with a clear theme; it illustrates science forging ahead against superstition, religious sanctions, cultural taboo, and even well-meaning but uneducated neighbors. Ogle takes this anecdote directly from Cuvier. In Cuvier's version, the story ends with Hippocrates

[18] Ogle 1882, 168.

declaring that Democritus is the wisest of men.[19] Ogle has slightly reordered the anecdote so that with the final words the emphasis is now on human bones ("quelques pieces ostéologiques"), and not Democritus. By retaining the original French–which was by no means necessary–he accentuates his punch line effect. Ogle is not writing as a scientist in this passage. He is a self-conscious stylist, not just reporting supporting data, but manipulating his material in the service of his point.

WILLIAM OGLE, TRANSLATOR OF *PARTS OF ANIMALS*

Who was William Ogle, and how did he happen upon Rokitansky's description of the puerperal osteophyte, which led him to postulate a potential resolution of a perplexing Aristotelian mistake? In the *Dictionary of British Classicists*[20] we learn that Ogle lived from 1827-1912, that he was trained as a doctor but practiced primarily as a teacher of physiology at St. George's Hospital, and that later he became the Superintendent of Statistics to the Registrar-General, a job he held for some 30 years.[21] In this capacity Ogle showed, like Aristotle himself, a talent for processing large quantities of data. The *Lives of the Fellows of the Royal College of Physicians* describes him as a "weighty contributor" to the *Journal of the Royal Statistical*

---

[19] Here is Cuvier's text: "Démocrite ne fut pas convenablement aprécié par ses compatriots. Errant souvant parmi les tombeaux, probablement pour y chercher quelques pieces ostéologiques, les Abdéritains imaginèrent qu'il avait l'esprit aliéné, et firent venir Hippocrate pour lui donner ses soins; mais ce grand homme ne vit rien moins qu'un fou dans Démocrite, et le déclara le plus sage et le plus savant des hommes," Cuvier 1970, 103.

[20] Todd 2004, 724-5.

[21] By a strange historical coincidence, a second William Ogle (1824-1905) was practicing medicine in London during this time, also at St. George's Hospital. Both William Ogles were graduates of Oxford. Interestingly enough, the William Ogle who translated Aristotle was not deemed worthy of an entry in Britain's *Dictionary of National Biography* (the claim to fame of Virginia Woolf's father, Sir Leslie Stephen), whereas the other William Ogle, a lecturer in pathology, was. It seems unlikely that the relative merit of their scholarly output was the decisive factor in including one William Ogle but not the other, given that the *Dictionary*'s entry lists only two publications for William Ogle: the "Harveian Oration" of 1880 at the Royal College of Physicians (of which the other William Ogle was also a member–indeed he may have been in the audience) and "a small work," *On the Relief of Excessive and Dangerous Tympanites by Puncture of the Abdomen* (p. 41).

Society.[22] His yearly reports for the Registrar-General included a variety of articles on such topics as vaccination, the increase in the incidence of cancer, and the age of marriage for bachelors in different occupations.[23] Ogle was responsible for a new kind of statistical table classifying causes of death (based on actual cause rather than pathology),[24] which may explain his familiarity with the discoveries of Rokitansky such as the puerperal osteophyte. He was also a botanist, and fluent enough in German to translate *Flowers and their Unbidden Guests* by Anton Kerner. This hobby led to correspondence with two of the most famous natural scientists of his time, the English botanist Joseph Hooker, and Charles Darwin, who wrote the introduction to Ogle's translation of Kerner's book.[25] Reading his obituary notices, one comes away with a sense of William Ogle as the quintessential Victorian gentleman scholar. Here is how the *Times* described the final years of his life:

> Of late years Dr. Ogle suffered very severely from osteo-arthritis, chiefly affecting the lower limbs and greatly crippling his movements; but as long as he was able to do so he was accustomed to drag himself into the Athenaem Club, and, once seated among friends, had the happy knack of forgetting, or of seeming to forget, sufferings which must often have been severe. Endeared to many, he

---

[22] Brown 1955, 155.

[23] See obituary notices in the *London Times* (April 15, 1912) and *Lancet* (April 27, 1912), and the *British Medical Journal* (April 20, 1912).

[24] *Lancet* 1912, 1165.

[25] *London Times*, op. cit. Existing correspondence between William Ogle and Charles Darwin covers the period from March 29, 1867 to April 12, 1882, seven days before Darwin's death on April 19. Summaries of these letters can be found online at <http://darwin.lib.cam.ac.uk/>. The subjects are wide-ranging and various. So, for example, in letter 10167 (September, 1875) Ogle asks Darwin whether Aristotle is correct when he observes that bees only visit a single type of flower in any given trip from their hive. In letter 8120 (December, 1871) Darwin sends a letter to Ogle with comments about left and right-handedness. The last two letters date to January, 1882 (letter 13622) in which Darwin thanks Ogle for sending his translation of *Parts of Animals*, and February, 1882 (letter 13697) where Darwin acknowledges having read Ogle's introduction and started the translation itself. "I have rarely read anything which has interested me more; though I have not read as yet more than a quarter of the book proper," he wrote.

> never willingly let an old acquaintance drop, and even in his last declining years, when to write a letter was an effort, he kept up his friendships by correspondence.[26]

It is somewhat astonishing that in the midst of such a busy life William Ogle would be able to find time to translate Aristotle's *Parts of Animals.* But it may be that this is how he occupied himself in the years between 1872, when he left his job at St George's Hospital for health reasons (not specified in any of the sources I consulted) and 1880, when he began his work for the Registrar-General's office.[27] Ogle's translation appeared in the first complete English edition of Aristotle's works prepared by J. A. Smith and W. D. Ross for Oxford, and is still in print today. In his preface to the updated *Complete Works of Aristotle* Jonathan Barnes writes, "The translators whom Smith and Ross collected together included the most eminent English Aristotelians of the age; and the translations reached a remarkable standard of scholarship and fidelity to the text."[28] A. L. Peck, who translated *Parts of Animals* for the bilingual Loeb edition, echoes Barnes' assessment of Ogle's work: "Any English translator must stand very much indebted to the work of William Ogle . . . It is not possible to overrate the care and exactness with which this piece of work was executed."[29] Of course, it was not only Ogle's careful translation which distinguished his *Parts of Animals*, it was also the copious notes that accompanied the text, notes influenced and shaped by Ogle's medical and scientific background. Like Mayhew, Ogle is interested in affirming the scientific accuracy (or conversely noting the inaccuracies) of what Aristotle wrote. However because, unlike Mayhew, Ogle's role is that of commentator, his authorial voice retains the stamp of his personal voice. As we have seen in his brief biography, Ogle is well positioned to avoid being caught in that uncomfortable gap that now exists, as noted by von Staden above, between science and classical philology.

---

[26] Ibid.

[27] In another striking coincidence, the other William Ogle also left his job at St. George's because of ill health. According to the *Dictionary of National Biography* this William Ogle resigned in 1876 because of depression, but was "cured shortly afterwards by an attack of enteric fever."

[28] Barnes 1984, ix.

[29] Peck 1961, 45.

KARL ROKITANSKY AND THE PUERPERAL OSTEOPHYTE

But how good is the science of William Ogle? The explanation of Aristotle's mistake concerning cranial sutures in men and women hinges upon Karl Rokitansky and the condition he named "puerperal osteophyte." Karl Rokitansky (1804-1878) is a fitting player in this Aristotelian puzzle, if only because his own life's work proved him to be true to the Aristotelian principle of grounding theory in careful observations of the real world. He was an early pathologist, working at the Vienna Medical School. In her history of the Vienna Medical School in the nineteenth century, Erna Lesky writes that Rokitansky's task was "to arouse German medicine from its natural-philosophical dream and to base it on solid, unchangeable, material facts."[30] Before Rokitansky, physicians approached illnesses through their symptoms.[31] Rokitansky's information, collected from an enormous number of autopsies (30,000 according to one source), allowed him to create a more coherent and systematic picture of various diseases.[32] Lesky describes his accomplishment in this way:

> In trying to realize the first point of his program, that of sorting and classifying the pathological disease products, Rokitansky immediately proved himself a born pathological anatomist. With sheer concentration on the senses which characterized his approach, he devoted himself to the visible and perceptible disease products. . . .

---

[30] Lesky 1976, 107. Interestingly enough, Erna Lesky provides a serendipitous link between Rokitansky and ancient Greek science, for in addition to her work on the history of medicine in the nineteenth century, she is the editor of Rokitansky's autobiography, and the author of numerous articles on ancient medicine. (Lesky is also the wife of classicist Albin Lesky, who wrote extensively on Greek tragedy.)

[31] Long 1928, 175: "After Rokitansky names of diseases, like pneumonia and typhoid fever, conveyed to the well trained medical graduate an anatomical picture and not as theretofore, a list of symptoms of varying complexity."

[32] Weyers 2004, 432. Weyers notes that while some physicians at that time questioned the value of autopsy, "Nobody did more to disprove those notions than Rokitansky who insisted that case histories be given together with the cadavers, who integrated clinical and pathologic findings, and who thus prepared the ground for the morphologic era in medicine."

> On the dissection table an objective picture of the disease emerged from thousands upon thousands of details.[33]

Rokitansky's legacy endures, represented by numerous pathological conditions that bear his name: Mayer-Rokitansky-Küster-Hauser syndrome (women born without a complete vagina), Rokitansky's diverticulum (an outpouching of the esophagus), and Rokitansky-Cushing ulcer (a bleeding problem in the intestines following trauma to the head), to list but three.[34] However, the puerperal osteophyte is not one of these.

What is the puerperal osteophyte, according to Rokitansky? He describes it as a layer of bone of varying thickness growing inside the skulls of women who died while pregnant.[35] Rokitansky was particularly excited about the connection between this abnormal bone growth and pregnancy:

> The exudation of bone, which is met with on the inner table of the skull in pregnant women, deserves an especial notice. It is so frequently observed in women under such circumstances, and advances in them to so great an extent, compared with what it reaches in other cases, that some connection between it and pregnancy must be admitted; and as it has been regarded with interest, since the time of its discovery in this institution [the Vienna Medical School], I devote the following paragraphs to an account of it.[36]

Although this growth is usually found on the inside of the skull,[37] it may appear outside the skull as well.[38] Rokitansky never explicitly

---

[33] Lesky 1976, 107-8.

[34] See <www.whonamedit.com/doctor.cfm/981.html>, which gives a partial list with descriptions.

[35] Rokitansky 1855, 111; 164-6.

[36] Ibid., 164.

[37] Ibid., 164: "Processes of this kind mostly take place on the inner table of the skull, and especially upon and near those spots which are best supplied with vessels; they are, therefore, common along the sinuses and the sutural margins of the bones, and furnish the bone at those parts with a new vitreous table."

[38] Ibid., 165-6: "When the exudation is more than usually thick and extensive, a similar, but thinner, stratum is found on the outer table of the

says that the puerperal osteophyte causes certain cranial sutures to disappear, nor does he make a specific distinction between the appearance of a skull with a puerperal osteophyte on the inside versus one on the outside. Logically, however, it seems that a bony growth on top of the cranial suture would be more likely to hide the suture from view than a growth below it. And, this external manifestation of the puerperal osteophyte is clearly less common according to Rokitansky, who qualifies the growth in this instance as "more than *usually* thick." So when William Ogle says that it is not "uncommon" for cranial sutures to become "more or less effaced" in pregnant women he might be pushing the evidence just a little bit. We could also quibble with the fact that Rokitansky describes the puerperal osteophyte as being deposited along the sagittal *and* the coronal sutures, whereas Ogle's solution to the Aristotelian puzzle requires the disappearance of the sagittal suture only. If the coronal suture is gone, there is no circle.

I will return to this problematic coronal suture presently, but in the meantime it must be noted that present day medicine seems to be entirely ignorant of Rokitansky's puerperal osteophyte. In modern medical terminology osteophytes are bone spurs that usually form along the joints.[39] A search of the medical databases for any research on puerperal osteophytes of the skull turned up exactly one article written in 1958. Of the nine references in this article's bibliography, one is to Rokitansky's manual, four cite the work of A. Hanau (all dated between 1892 and 1894), and the dates of the remaining references are: 1901, 1933, 1935, and 1952. The bulk of the data therefore comes from the nineteenth century when information about the skull and what is inside it would come primarily from autopsies. My, admittedly unscientific, survey of physicians (including an Emergency Room physician, an obstetrician/gynecologist, a pathologist, a surgeon and a professor of anatomy) found no one who had ever heard of the puerperal osteophyte. I do not want to suggest that it has never existed. In fact, Haslhofer's 1958 article includes two pictures of this condition. But although the puerperal osteophyte may

---

skull: at this part, also, as on the inner table, it appears to select the frontal and parietal bones, and *is deposited chiefly along the coronal and sagittal sutures*, and along the part at which the temporal muscle is attached, and the linea semicircularis; it may even be found on the external surface of the bones of the face, especially on the superior maxillary and nasal." [Emphasis added.]

[39] *Dorland's Illustrated Medical Dictionary* 2000, 1290.

have been common at one time, it certainly does not appear to be so now. In fact, even as early as 1875, one pathology manual, having described the condition *per* Rokitansky, then asserts, "But the connection of this growth with the puerperal state is very doubtful."[40] Is it possible that this condition, because it is benign, has simply become irrelevant to modern medicine? Could it have largely disappeared because of environmental changes, or changes in nutrition and management of pregnancy? Given the detail with which science is now able to map out the human body, inside and out, the apparent total disappearance of the puerperal osteophyte is perplexing. Consequently, what was an interesting speculation on Ogle's part is ultimately a problematic way to account for Aristotle's mistaken description of human cranial sutures. The puerperal osteophyte theory is at home in Ogle's commentary, but it sits uncomfortably in Mayhew's attempt to show an absence of gender bias in Aristotle's biology.

Moreover, there are several small flaws in Ogle's reasoning that undermine his speculation from the beginning. The first part of his note on this passage in *Parts of Animals* (not quoted in Mayhew's excerpt) explains that Aristotle correctly identifies the number of sutures in his account of the male skull as three–the sagittal and the two arms of the lambdoid–because he considers the coronal suture to be part of the bones of the face, not the skull. Logically then, if Aristotle really did see a skull that seemed to have no sagittal suture down the middle, he would not have described it as having a singular circular suture if he counted the coronal suture as belonging to the bones of the face and not the skull. In the absence of a sagittal suture, Aristotle should have described the sutures of this putative female skull as two in number, i.e. the two arms of the lambdoid suture. The fact that Aristotle's description of the male skull emphasizes the angularity of the lambdoid suture to the extent of counting it as two different sutures also raises the issue that if Aristotle did see a female skull with what looked like a singular circular suture, it would require not only that he consider the coronal suture as belonging to the skull rather than the face in the case of women but not in men–a troubling inconsistency–but also that the two arms of the lambdoid suture must somehow be flattened out enough to no longer look like two separate sutures.

[40] Jones and Sieveking 1875, 854.

A FOOTNOTE FUGUE

These problems are of course missing from Mayhew's argument, nor do they seem to have come to the attention of the scholars Mayhew footnotes in support of his position that Ogle's theory of the puerperal osteophyte provides a plausible explanation for Aristotle's mistake concerning human cranial sutures. I now propose a close examination of the references Mayhew cites, some of which come with interesting footnotes of their own. Reading these responses to Aristotle's mistake produces what we might characterize as a footnote *fugue*: the various voices echo each other, sometimes exactly and sometimes with subtle modulations, but always keeping Ogle's commentary as a primary theme.

Mayhew's citation of Lesley Dean-Jones references her book, *Women's Bodies in Classical Greek Science.* Dean-Jones' mention of cranial sutures occurs in her chapter titled "Female Anatomy and Physiology" under the rubric "External Genitalia." (This sounds stranger than it actually is.) The context is a discussion of the Hippocratic position that the vagina and the urethra were two separate organs, contrasted with Aristotle's belief that they were a single organ. Dean-Jones cites a passage from the Hippocratic corpus on the subject of the urethra in men and women whose manuscript tradition is problematic. She then goes on to explain:

> If the confusion in the manuscripts is due to a later interpolation, it could be attributed to the influence of Aristotle, because he failed to recognize the separation of the urethra and the vagina. *This is a direct result of one of the founding principles of Aristotle's biology: that the female is a less perfect representative of the human form than the male. The same principle led him to make other erroneous claims.*[41]

Dean-Jones then inserts a brief discussion of the cranial sutures mistake, followed by a similarly brief treatment of Aristotle's declaration that women have fewer teeth than men, before returning to her main topic, namely Aristotle's failure to distinguish between the urethra and the vagina. Here is Dean-Jones' conclusion:

[41] Dean-Jones 1994, 81 [emphasis added].

> [Aristotle's] usually astute readings in contemporary medical literature should also have suggested this anatomical fact to him. Aristotle did not assimilate this knowledge because what would here seem to be a legitimate difference between man and woman, unlike the spurious differences he lists elsewhere, would make a woman superior in some respect by the further specialization of her body to separate her two fluid residues. This is one difference Aristotle simply failed to register because he did not expect it or think of looking for it: it went against one of his most basic tenets.[42]

Skull sutures and teeth presumably fall into the category of "spurious differences," but Dean-Jones might also be thinking of them as spurious *mistakes*, since in each instance she supplies a plausible explanation: Ogle's theory of the puerperal osteophyte for cranial sutures,[43] and in the case of dental differences, her suggestion that by sheer coincidence Aristotle just happened to look in the mouths of women who had fewer teeth.[44] By including these particular mistakes–which may, in fact, not have been mistakes–Dean-Jones reinforces her observation of cultural gender bias behind a more significant mistake: Aristotle's assumption that women could not have had two separate organs (urethra and vagina) when men only had one. In other words, Dean-Jones uses the cranial sutures mistake to throw into higher relief a mistake that, in her opinion *cannot* be easily explained away.

Let us look at exactly how Dean-Jones presents Ogle's theory as a way to explain Aristotle's remarks about cranial sutures in humans. Here is the passage in full; I have intercalated Dean-Jones' footnotes.

> [Aristotle] states that a man has more sutures in his skull because he has a bigger brain and a bigger brain needs more ventilation. [Footnote 131: *PA* 653a27-9, 653b1-3.] Men and women have the same number of sutures in their

[42] Ibid., 83. Mayhew, needless to say, does not include this Aristotelian mistake in his study.

[43] Ibid., 81.

[44] Ibid., 82. Fewer teeth might be explained by the absence of wisdom teeth, for example. Mayhew does include a discussion of teeth in his study, pp. 81-86.

> skulls, so it may seem as if here Aristotle is citing completely non-existent evidence as proof of the male's superiority over the female. However at *HA* 491b3-5 he enumerates the sutures as three in a man and one circular one in a woman. Ogle records, "it is by no means uncommon for the sutures on the vertex to become more or less effaced in pregnant women; so common is it, that the name 'puerperal osteophyte' has been given to the condition by Rokitansky." [Footnote 132: Ogle 1882, 168.] In this condition the sagittal suture disappears and the lamboid [*sic*], lateral, and coronal sutures form a circle. Aristotle may have seen or heard of such a skull and, as it was different from a *normal* skull (perhaps seen most commonly on battlefields and therefore easily identified as male), explained its unusual features by saying it was female, even if he did not know for a fact that it was a woman's skull. [Emphasis added.][45]

There are several things worth noticing in Dean-Jones' version of the cranial sutures problem. First, the quotation from Ogle is fairly opaque until it is explained in the sentence that follows ("In this condition the sagittal suture disappears and the lamboid [*sic*], lateral, and coronal sutures form a circle").[46] If we were to place this passage in Dean-Jones side by side with Ogle's original note we would find that the placement of her footnote citing Ogle is slightly off. Both the anatomical explanation (i.e., the naming of the sutures and the description of the process whereby a circle appears) as well as the reference to finding male skulls on battlefields, properly belong to Ogle. Dean-Jones, rather than choose between quotation and paraphrase–the two options footnoting allows–has used both, but her paraphrase remains outside the footnote, and thus unattributed to Ogle. In the greater scheme of things such a minor slippage is of little importance, but in this case there is a small but significant repercussion that colors the way we read this passage. If Dean-Jones had quoted Ogle in full, as Mayhew does, we would have before us a theory about the circular cranial suture based upon nineteenth-century gynecological pathology. As it stands however, Dean-Jones

[45] Op. cit.

[46] In the interest of scientific accuracy, it should be noted that there is no cranial suture named "lateral."

has essentially moved the medical explanation into the 20th century when those words ("the sagittal suture disappears" etc.) become hers and not William Ogle's. In so doing she has finessed what, given the scientific advances that separate 19th and 20th century medicine, is a problematically large body of knowledge.

In addition, Dean-Jones raises the issue of *how* Aristotle knew the skull with only one singular suture had belonged to a woman. Ogle does not directly address this question. Mayhew takes for granted that Aristotle knew it came from a woman who died while pregnant or in childbirth. Dean-Jones, on the other hand, speculates that Aristotle may have simply decided that a skull that was markedly different from all the others he had seen—assuming, with Ogle, that most of these would have been from battle casualties and thus male—would have to be female, as a way to account for that difference. This theory is somewhat compromised by the fact that in the *History of Animals*, in both passages that mention gender difference in cranial sutures (1.7 and 3.7), after claiming that the skulls of women have a single circular suture Aristotle adds that a man's head has been found with no sutures at all.[47] We do not know how Aristotle knew that this strange skull belonged to a man (unless he is simply taking Herodotus' word for it), but this piece of evidence weakens Dean-Jones' suggestion that a skull with an unusual appearance was identified as female *because* of that unusual appearance, and not because Aristotle had managed to get his hands on a female skull. More telling is the adjective Dean-Jones chooses to make her point. Aristotle, she says, may have found a skull that was not "normal" and accounted for this abnormality by labeling it female. By switching the terms of the gender comparison: more (skull sutures and teeth) = superior vs. fewer = inferior, to the opposition of normal and abnormal, Dean-Jones subtly takes us back to her main underlying theme, that for Aristotle, a woman was essentially a mutilated man, a man missing something.[48]

---

[47] ἤδη δ' ὤφθη καὶ ἀνδρὸς κεφαλὴ οὐκ ἔχουσα ῥαφάς. (The skull of a man was also seen before now having no sutures.) Commentators (A. L. Peck for the Loeb edition, e.g.) point out that Herodotus (with his characteristic interest in the wondrous and strange) describes a skull with no sutures having been found on the battlefield of Plataea (*Histories*, 9.83) along with a jawbone with the teeth growing together in a single piece and an extremely tall skeleton. Aristotle may have been thinking about this passage.

[48] Dean-Jones quotes this passage in a later section on reproduction (p. 182). The passage is from Aristotle's *Generation of Animals*, 737a28: τὸ γὰρ θῆλυ

The text by G. E. R. Lloyd cited in Mayhew's footnote is *Science, Folklore and Ideology*.[49] Lloyd's treatment of the cranial sutures mistake occurs in a paragraph that begins with the following sentence: "The correlations [Aristotle] expects lead him, also, to a number of superficial and some quite inaccurate statements on anatomical points which it should not have been too hard to check."[50] Notice that in spite of the remonstrative tone, Aristotle is not the agent in this sentence. He is the object of the verb, manipulated into error as it were by his expected correlations. Lloyd then names four mistakes: first, the assertion that men have more teeth; next, that they have more cranial sutures; finally Aristotle's claim that males have bigger brains, and, in a footnote to this last point, the "further claim" that males have harder bones. Here is how Lloyd presents the cranial sutures mistake, with his footnotes intercalated, as above:

> Again it would not have been impossible for [Aristotle] to have carried out the observations that would have revealed the incorrectness of his assertion that men have more sutures on the skull than women. He represents the latter as having a singular circular suture [Footnote 165: *HA* 491b2ff, 516a18ff. D' A. W. Thompson 1910, notes to *HA* ad loc., suggests that Aristotle may have imagined that the sutures correspond to partings in the hair. Ogle 1882, p. 168 n. 26, notes that "the opportunities of seeing a female skull would be much fewer than of seeing a male skull; for battle-fields would no longer be of service." Compare the account of the different configurations of the sutures in *VC* ch. I, L III 182.1ff, and cf. Galen *UP* IX 17, II 49.26ff H, K III 751.7ff.]–a doctrine that corresponds to the view that males are hotter than females, for the sutures have the function of cooling the brain and providing it with ventilation. [Footnote 166: *PA* 653b2f.][51]

ὥσπερ ἄρρεν ἐστὶ πεπηρωμένον. (For the female, as it were, is a mutilated male.) The verb I have translated as "mutilated" can specifically indicate castration, but it can also mean to be defective or incapacitated. Dean-Jones translates as "deformed."

[49] Lloyd 1983.

[50] Ibid., 102.

[51] Ibid.

Lloyd assumes that Aristotle should have been able to correct this mistake with more careful observation, although his phrasing implicitly acknowledges that it would have been more difficult than counting teeth. Curiously, his reference to Ogle in his footnote omits any mention of the puerperal osteophyte scenario and notes only Ogle's speculation that Aristotle probably did not see many female skulls. (Few opportunities, we are to understand, is equivalent to, "It would not have been impossible . . .") Lloyd's omission of the puerperal osteophyte suggests that he preferred Thompson's explanation–quoted by Mayhew, but not by Dean-Jones–of why Aristotle would have described the skull's sutures as he did: namely that the sutures follow the pattern of hair partings. Thompson's theory will be addressed in detail presently. For the moment I note what strikes me as problematic in Lloyd's footnote. Certainly it makes intuitive sense to see a central part as corresponding to the sagittal suture, and the hairline going around the head as corresponding to a single 'circular' suture. But if Aristotle were thinking in these terms then that would mean that he believed that women were physiologically incapable of parting their hair in the middle! This seems quite implausible. In fact many Greek female statues dating from the Archaic *kore* figures depict a central hair parting. By introducing a connection between skull sutures and hair Lloyd sidesteps the problem of Aristotle's description of a *gendered* difference in human skull sutures, because the difference is skulls is now a question of where the hair parts naturally, regardless of sex. This move is reinforced by the other references cited in his footnote: the Hippocratic text *Wounds of the Head* ("VC") and Galen's *De Usu Partium.* Neither work–Galen is essentially quoting the earlier Hippocratic text–mentions gender difference, but rather each describes the skull sutures in terms of various Greek letters (*tau, eta,* and *chi*), depending upon the shape of the head.

Aside from Thompson, Mayhew's final reference in his footnote is to the translation and commentary on *Parts of Animals* by James Lennox.[52] Checking the passage in question we find that like Ogle, Lennox feels that Aristotle's remark that the skulls of men have more cranial sutures than those of women calls for some additional information. He writes:

[52] Lennox 2001.

> The differences between the sutures of male and female humans, and between humans and other animals, are repeatedly discussed in *History of Animals.* These claims are false, but their specificity argues for their being based on some sort of observation (for a speculation, see Ogle 1882: 168 n. 26; 1912: 653bI nn. 3, 4). None the less, it has been argued that Aristotle's theory of the cooling function of the sutures may have led to the uncritical adoption of such claims (Lloyd 1983: 102 and nn. 165-7; 1989a: 57).[53]

As we might expect in a commentary, Lennox begins by pointing out that Aristotle also talks about gender difference in cranial sutures in a second text, i.e., *History of Animals.* It is in this text, we recall, that Aristotle specifically mentions a singular suture in human female skulls. As for the puerperal osteophyte theory behind the circular suture, Lennox's note qualifies Ogle's hypothesis as a "speculation" and omits the medical particulars, preferring instead to insist upon the fact that the details (i.e., a single *circular* suture vs. three that meet at a point) imply that Aristotle is basing his observation upon something he (or someone else) saw. In other words, he indicates that an ideologically driven description might have simply noted fewer sutures in women's skulls, but not necessarily a single circular one.

However, Lennox is clearly not satisfied that Aristotle has been completely exonerated of ideological bias, so he adds, "it has been argued" that Aristotle's point about the circular suture is driven by a theory–that the function of cranial sutures is to cool the brain–and is thus an "uncritical adoption" of the claim that female human skulls have fewer sutures. Note that here Lennox is carefully suggesting that Aristotle probably did not see such a skull himself, but was told about it by another observer, and accepted this observation as factual because it cohered with his idea about the function of cranial sutures. Support for this proposition is provided by a reference to Lloyd's text, which we have just examined. Interestingly, Lennox avoids any mention of gender at this point, and the cooling function theory is not, in and of itself, an example of Aristotelian gender bias. The bias comes into play only when coupled with Aristotle's assumption that men's brains need more cooling (and thus more sutures) because they are bigger and hotter than women's brains. The problem of misogynistic preconception on the part of Aristotle, while not

[53] Ibid., 209-10.

eliminated completely, has been very subtly sanitized in Lennox's note, having been recast as an issue of a mistaken theory about the function of cranial sutures, with gender difference left implicitly in the background.

RECAPPING

Reviewing Mayhew's cited sources in terms of narrative choices, here is what we have found. He has truncated Ogle's note to emphasize both the probable scarcity of female skulls available to Aristotle for observation, and Rokitansky's puerperal osteophyte condition, which could explain the appearance of a circular suture in female skulls. Mayhew leaves out Ogle's reminder at the beginning of his note that for Aristotle the coronal suture belongs to the bones of the face, and thus does not confront the problem that his male skull, with its three sutures, does not count the coronal suture, whereas the female skull, with its circular suture, does. He also leaves out–as one would expect him to–the final part of Ogle's note in which Ogle presents us (courtesy of Cuvier) with two anecdotes from antiquity illustrating the point that access to information about the inside of the human body was difficult at best for ancient scientists. This information is not necessary for Mayhew's argument. Indeed restoring Ogle's note in full reveals, as we have seen, a very different kind of discourse, one that if reproduced in Mayhew's citation would be in direct competition with the scientific discourse characterizing the beginning of the note. It is precisely because they represent a different kind of discourse that Ogle's stories about Galen and Democritus have the potential to destabilize the scientific edifice that Mayhew is in the process of constructing.

Supporting this edifice is a footnote that references Lesley Dean-Jones, G. E. R. Lloyd, and James Lennox. The presence of Dean-Jones in Mayhew's note is a powerful reminder of the ability of the footnote to subsume the individual voice in the service of consensus. Although Dean-Jones uses Ogle's note in a way that is quite similar to Mayhew's, she and Mayhew are in fact operating with *opposing* agendas. Whereas Mayhew wants to assert a minimum of gender bias in Aristotle's biological writings, Dean-Jones insists upon it. In her text the cranial sutures mistake serves as a reminder that in spite of the fact that Aristotle's scientific accuracy may be greater than he is given credit for, this accuracy cannot efface his mistaken notion that woman was essentially an inferior version of man. Unlike Dean-

Jones, Lloyd and Lennox both avoid the details of Ogle's puerperal osteophyte theory–for Lennox, we recall, it is a "speculation," and Lloyd does not mention it at all–and both take on the problem of gender bias in a rather oblique way, carefully subordinating the cranial sutures mistake to a larger theoretical picture that includes the function of cranial sutures. Technically then, neither offers strong support for Mayhew's argument, although there is no way to know that; their presence at the bottom of the page is sufficient for his purposes.

CODA. CRANIAL SUTURES AND HAIR PARTINGS

D'Arcy W. Thompson's 1910 translation and commentary of *History of Animals* was included–along with Ogle's translation of *Parts of Animals*–in the Oxford edition of the complete works of Aristotle.[54] Unsurprisingly Thompson found the two references in *History of Animals* to women having a single circular cranial suture (vs. three sutures for men) both worthy of comment. His note on 1.7, quoted in Mayhew's footnote, reads:

> CF. *H.A.* [*History of Animals*] iii.7.516a19 [Book 3, chapter 7] (and note), *P.A.* [*Parts of Animals*] 11.10.656b14. I imagine that this singular misstatement dates from a belief that the sutures of the skull coincided with the margin and the partings of the hairy scalp.[55]

Thompson's later note on Aristotle's repeated mention of gender difference in skull sutures at 3.7 observes the following:

> The alleged difference between the male and female skull is one of the puzzles of Aristotelian anatomy; I am inclined to think (with Harduin, *ad* Plin. xi. 48) that A. imagined the sutures to correspond with the partings of the hair, but see Ogle's note (*Parts of Anim.* P. 168).[56]

[54] Completed in 1954 under the editorial direction of J. A. Smith and W. D. Ross. The entire collection was revised under the editorship of Jonathan Barnes, published in 1984.
[55] Thompson 1910 (pages not numbered).
[56] Ibid.

A connection between cranial sutures and the hair on the head does make sense from Aristotle's point of view. Here is how he describes it in *Parts of Animals*, in William Ogle's translation:

> No animal has so much hair on the head as man. This in the first place is the necessary result of the fluid character of his brain, and of the presence of so many sutures in his skull. For wherever there is the most fluid and the most heat, there must necessarily occur the greatest outgrowth.[57]

Thompson must be inferring that if the sutures allow the fluid of the brain to escape, that is where we would find hair growth demarcated. However, as I have noted above, is a strange way to account for a *gendered* difference in human skulls. Aristotle does not discuss gender differentiation in the pattern of hair growth in humans. Can Pliny, whom Thompson credits (via Harduin) as responsible for this idea, resolve the dilemma?

Pliny the Elder was a Roman scholar (he died during the eruption of Mt. Vesuvius in 79 CE) very much in the Aristotelian mold, inasmuch as he was a prodigious collector and sorter of information of all types. The scale of his coverage as well as the assortment of facts is astonishing.[58] The primary subject announced for Book XI, where we find the passage referenced by Thompson, is "types of insects," which seems at the outset to be an extremely odd place to find information about human cranial sutures. However the particular subject discussed in Chapter 48 belongs to a section where Pliny gives an account of the nature of all animals by taking each organ or part separately, the skull being one of those parts. Here is the full text of Chapter 48, in Rackham's Loeb translation, with the relevant sentence underlined and accompanied by Pliny's own words in Latin:

> In human beings only a double-crowned skull occurs in some cases. <u>The bones of the human skull are flat and thin and have no marrow; they are constructed with interlockings serrated like the teeth of a comb</u> [*Capitis ossa plana, tenuis, sine medullis, serratis pectinatim structa compagibus.*]

---

[57] Ogle 1882, 49.

[58] Book 1, which contains the table of contents for the remaining 36 books as well as Pliny's sources, takes up 143 pages in the Loeb translation. Rackham, 1938.

> When broken they cannot form again, but the removal of a moderate piece is not fatal, as its place is taken by a scar of flesh. The skull of the bear is the weakest and that of the parrot the hardest, as we have stated in the proper place.[59]

The closest thing to "partings of the hairy scalp" in this passage is the adverb *pectinatim*, "like a comb" (from the Latin noun for "comb," *pectin*), which describes the appearance of the skull sutures, not their location. (Pliny does go on to discuss hair in a later chapter.)

Thompson gives credit to Harduin for the hair partings theory, so the error may have originated in Harduin's reading of Pliny. Who was Harduin? Jean Hardouin[60] was a French scholar (1649-1729) who edited an edition of Pliny's *Natural History*.[61] Hardouin's editorial comment on the passage cited above (where Pliny says that the bones of the skull are *serratis pectinatim*, serrated like a comb) addresses the word "serrated." He writes: *Suturas intellegit; in mulieribus una est in orbem; in viris, ternae* [He (Pliny) means sutures; in women there is a single one in a circle; in men there are three]. In other words, Hardouin glosses the Pliny passage–where there is no mention of either hair or gender difference–with a reference to what Aristotle says about gender difference in cranial sutures in *History of Animals* (1.7 and 3.7), a passage where there is also no mention of hair. Thompson's idea, which makes sense from the Aristotelian perspective of the relationship between hair and skull sutures, makes no sense from the perspective of gender difference in skull sutures. And Thompson's supporting footnote, which directs us to Hardouin and his primary source, Pliny, gets us no closer to hair partings than the mention of the teeth of a comb.

CONCLUSION

Commentary, to paraphrase Christina Kraus, takes as its starting point the "disorder" created by a problem in a primary text

59 Ibid., 515.

60 Thompson's misspelling of his name is explained by the fact that in Hardouin's edition of Pliny his name would have appeared on the title page in a Latinate version, without the "o."

61 The edition I consulted, from the library of the Merkelbeek Carmelite Monastery, was published from 1829-1834 with, in addition to Hardouin's notes, those of (unnamed) more recent scholars (*et recentiorum adnotationibus*).

and then imposes order in an explanatory "meta-narrative."[62] Ogle's note on Aristotle's mistaken observation that men have three cranial sutures while women have only one demonstrates this principle beautifully. Ogle gives us a scenario that explains circumstances under which Aristotle might have legitimately made this false claim. Mayhew takes this meta-narrative and places it in the service of an argument, namely that Aristotle was not, in the case of cranial sutures, simply making a claim that reflected the gender bias of his time and place. This process produces a footnote referencing other Aristotelian scholars, all of whom mention Ogle in one way or another. By letting these secondary texts speak fully in their own voices, I have essentially offered a commentary of Mayhew's footnote, generating a new meta-narrative. Kraus described the meta-narrative of commentary as corresponding to a potential *mise en abyme.* The meta-narrative of my commentary, on the other hand, inscribes a different path corresponding–although perhaps in a different way–to the "ludic" principle mentioned by Kraus. Rather than a progression of infinite regression it creates an ever-expanding web of connections in an outward spiral. Anthony Grafton, at the end of *The Footnote,* uses similar imagery, evoking the weaving of Homer's Penelope:

> Wise historians know that their craft resembles Penelope's art of weaving: footnotes and text will come together again and again, in ever-changing combinations of patterns and colors. Stability is not to be reached. Nonetheless, the culturally contingent and eminently fallible footnote offers the only guarantee we have that statements about the past derive from identifiable sources. And that is the only ground we have to trust them.[63]

In other words, the puerperal osteophyte may have disappeared from the medical world, but Rokitansky and his observations will always have a place in the history of Aristotelian scholarship. Similarly, Hardouin may not have been responsible for a theory that successfully brought together gender difference in cranial sutures and the partings of the hair, but he nevertheless will always remain a member of our scholarly community. He is, in the words of Grafton, an "identifiable source." To that extent, Thompson's note citing

[62] Kraus 2002, 9, quoted in the introductory section of this essay.
[63] Grafton 1997, 233.

Hardouin is indeed trustworthy. But Hardouin may not be. He has the dubious honor of having proposed a theory that most surviving texts from antiquity (Pliny's *Natural History* was of course an exception) were not authentic, as we learn from one of his contemporaries, Johann Burkhard Mencken (1674-1732), in a lecture series titled, "The Charlatanry of the Learned":

> So far I have spoken only of authors who are dead, and I hesitate to speak of one still alive–one who is today a light of learning in France, the Jesuit Jean Hardouin. He has already published a number of works worthy of remembrance, one alone of which, his "Pliny," is sufficient to immortalize him. But whether to amuse himself or, as some think, to attract attention to his society, he has attempted to establish the principle that the majority of the works that have come down to us from ancient times, ecclesiastical as well as secular, were produced, or at least altered, by a confederation of forgers. When pressed to give his reasons for this strange idea, he replies that as long as he lives God alone will know them, but that after he is dead they will be found on a piece of paper no larger than his hand. What an answer! I leave it to you to judge what it is worth.[64]

In the matrix that is the footnote, the web of connections has the potential to be endless, and it is our job to judge what they are worth.

BIBLIOGRAPHY

Anon. "Obituary." *Lancet* 84 (April 27, 1912): 1164-5.

———. "Obituary." *British Medical Journal* 1 (April 20, 1912): 929-30.

Aristotle. *Parts of Animals.* Translated by A. L. Peck. Cambridge, MA: Harvard University Press, 1961.

Barnes, Jonathan. *Aristotle. A Very Short Introduction.* Oxford: Oxford University Press, 2000.

[64] Mencken 1937, 82-3.

———. *The Complete Works of Aristotle.* Princeton: Princeton University Press, 1984.

Blum, Deborah. *Sex on the Brain.* New York: Viking Press, 1997.

Bourgey, Louis. *Observation et Expérience chez Aristote.* Paris: J. Vrin, 1955.

Brown, G. H. *Lives of the Fellows of the Royal College of Physicians of London1826-1925.* London: Published by the College, 1955.

Cuvier, Georges. *Histoire des sciences naturelles, depuis leur origine jusqu'à nos jours chez tous les peuples connus professée au Collège de France.* Westmead, England: Gregg International Publishers. 1970.

The Darwin Correspondence Online Database. <http://darwin.lib.cam.ac.uk/ (accessed December 14, 2006)>.

Dean-Jones, Leslie. *Women's Bodies in Classical Greek Science.* Oxford: Clarendon Press, 1994.

Dorland's Illustrated Medical Dictionary. Philadelphia: W. B. Saunders, 2000.

Grafton, Anthony. *The Footnote. A Curious History.* Cambridge, MA: Harvard University Press, 1997.

Haslhofer, L. "Zur Kenntnis des Schwangerschafts-Osteophyts am Schädeldach." *Wiener Klinische Wochenschrift* 70 (17), April 25, 1958.

Jones, Charles Handfield and Edward Henry Sieveking. *A Manual of Pathological Anatomy.* Philadelphia: Lindsay, 1875.

Kraus, Christina Shuttleworth. "Introduction: Reading Commentaries/Commentaries as Reading." In *The Classical Commentary. Histories, Practices, Theory*, edited by Roy K. Gibson and Christina Shuttleworth Kraus, 1-27. Leiden: Brill, 2002.

Kurtz, Donna C. and John Boardman. *Greek Burial Customs.* London: Thames and Hudson, 1971.

Lee, Sidney, ed. *The Dictionary of National Biography. Supplement, Jan. 1901-Dec. 1911*, vol. III. Oxford: Oxford University Press, 1920.

Lennox, James G., trans. *On the Parts of Animals.* Oxford: Clarendon Press, 2001.

———. "Demarcating Ancient Science." In *Oxford Studies in Ancient Philosophy*, vol. 3, edited by Julia Annas, 307-324. Oxford: Clarendon Press, 1985.

Lesky, Erna. *The Vienna Medical School of the 19th Century.* Baltimore: Johns Hopkins University Press, 1976.

Lewes, George Henry. *Aristotle: A Chapter from the History of Science.* London: Smith, Elder and Co., 1864.

Lloyd, G. E. R. *Science, Folklore and Ideology*. Cambridge: Cambridge University Press, 1983.

London Times. 1912. Obituaries, Dr. William Ogle, April 15.

Long, Esmond R. *A History of Pathology*. Baltimore: Williams & Wilkins, 1928.

Mayhew, Robert. *The Female in Aristotle's Biology. Reason or Rationalization*. Chicago: University of Chicago Press, 2004.

Mencken, Johann Burkhard. *The Charlatanry of the Learned (De Charlataneria Eruditorum, 1715) by Johann Burkhard Mencken (1674-1732), Translated from the Latin by Francis E. Litz, with Notes and an Introduction by H. L. Mencken*. New York: A. A. Knopf, 1937.

Nuñez-Ferandez, David, MD, PhD and Henry S. Schutta, MD. "Karl Freiheir van Rokintansky." *Who Named It?* <http://www.whonamedit.com/doctor.cfm/981.html>, (accessed August 15, 2006).

Ogle, William, trans. *Aristotle on* The Parts of Animals. London: Kegan Paul, Trench & Co., 1882.

Passingham, Richard. *What is Special about the Human Brain?* Oxford: Oxford University Press, 2008.

Pliny, the Elder. *Caii Plinii Secundi Historia Naturalis / ex recensione I. Harduini et recentiorum adnotationibus*. Turin: Augustae Taurinorum, 1829–1834.

Pliny, the Elder. , *Natural History*. Translated by H. Rackham. Cambridge, MA. Harvard University Press, 1938.

Rokitansky, Carl. *A Manual of Pathological Anatomy*. Translated by Charles Hewitt Moore. Philadelphia: Blanchard & Lea, 1855.

Russell, Bertrand. *Unpopular Essays*. New York: Simon and Schuster, 1951.

Stevens, Anne H. and Jay Williams. "The Footnote, in Theory." *Critical Inquiry* 32 no. 2 (2006): 208-225.

Thompson, D'Arcy Wentworth, trans. *Historia Animalium*. Oxford: Clarendon Press, 1910.

Todd, Robert B., ed. *The Dictionary of British Classicists*. Bristol: Thoemmes Continuum, 2004.

von Staden, Heinrich. "'A Woman Does not Become Ambidextrous': Galen and the Culture of Scientific Commentary." In *The Classical Commentary. Histories, Practices, Theory*, edited by Roy K. Gibson and Christina Shuttleworth Kraus 109-139. Leiden: Brill, 2002.

Weyers, Wolfgang, MD. "Carl Rokitansky: His Life, Work, and Contributions to Dermatopathology on the Occasion of his

200th Birthday." *American Journal of Dermatopathology* 26, no. 5 (2004): 431-438.

Barbara Clayton (MA French, Princeton; PhD Classics, Stanford) specializes in the poetry of Homer, with a particular emphasis on gender, psychoanalysis, and the Classical tradition. She is the author of *A Penelopean Poetics: Reweaving the Feminine in Homer's* Odyssey. Recent research resulted in "Polyphemus and Odysseus in the Nursery: Symbiosis and Semiotics in *Odyssey* 9," which is presently under consideration for publication. Currently she is teaching part-time at Stanford and working on a manuscript that takes as its point of departure the last book of the *Odyssey*.

KINESIS OF NOTHING AND THE *OUSIA* OF POETICS (PART REVIEW ESSAY, PART NOTES ON A POETICS OF AUTO-COMMENTARY)

Daniel C. Remein

Wildfire: A Verse Essay on Obscurity and Illumination. Brady, Andrea. San Francisco: Krupskaya, 2010. [Paperbound] 79pp. ISBN 978-1-92860-31-7.

i.

Andrea's Brady's relatively recent book *Wildfire: A Verse Essay on Obscurity and Illumination* contains Brady's own "Note On the Text" at the end of the book, which before anything else, explains that "*Wildfire* is a verse essay" (71). And then Brady explains that the book's primary concern involves what at first glance appears as a material history of *fire* (defined in a flickeringly multivalent and capacious manner):

> It [the book] is trying to persuade us, to recognize that certain catastrophes and felicities are not inevitable. It concerns the history of incendiary devices, of the evolution of Greek fire from a divine secret which could sustain or destroy empires, into white phosphorous and napalm; the elliptical fires of the pre-Socratics, Aristotle's service to Alexander in the fashioning of pyrotechnics . . . [of] mechanisms to project fire, to make it burn on water and stick to wood and skin, the keep if off the walls of besieged towns, and what those mechanisms (projection and defense) have done to geometry . . . (71)

Brady's list of these combustions, which she says drive her book, continues. The organization of this list seems to hover not only around a particular distaste for assuming that the inevitability of this history (or what or what certain theoretical discussions would refer to as the *necessity* of a history) is so driven, but also a desire or even a hope that one might somehow, even with writing, intervene in it: "I was tired of trying to position 'us' on the ground, like actors in real carnage, where being 'implicated' is also a way of sharing the spoils. I wanted not allegory but the recovery of material history" (71). And yet Brady does not allow her book or her readers the simple escape to a paranoid criticism which would assume that to shed light on this history would effectively expose its contingencies, or 'do enough' to look for alternatives. Rather, she implies that the wildfire she writes with is not merely a 'material' phenomenon–no matter how material its history–but one that, following those "elliptical fires of the pre-Socratics" is an elemental problem which, whether counted with the causes or the results of history, spreads hungrily into whatever comes to appearance.

For Brady the writing that would write of such a history must reckon with its own elemental relation to fire. Recalling the old convention of an ocular poetics and epistemology, Brady raises the figure of the firelight of exegesis and commentary, and investigates how they produce the flames whose light illuminates a text, what they burn, and what their smoke obscures–if in fact they do not consume the text to which they bring light. So as much as the book attempts to produce and inhabit "an etiology of [fire] metaphors, 'shake-n-bake' and whiskey pete and phantom fury," the book is also an auto-commentary, setting out to gloss such fire with additional fire, with the burning light of commentary and the darkness of its collateral effects: "It is also an argument about obscurity and illumination: WP [white phosphorous] does both, smokes the bright air and singes the night with trajectories. And so an interrogation of writings which fume as much as they enlighten" (71).

The book itself appeared first as a hypertext poem at *Dispatx.com*, cross-referencing and glossing its various citations, a veritable auto-glossed edition.[1] More directly, Brady elaborates the link between

The author wishes to thank several persons without whom this essay could not have been written: Ada Smailbegović and Meagan Manas for careful and sustained reading and comment on this essay as it developed; Jeff T. Johnson and Claire Donato, for productive conversation concerning the 'verse-essay' and the problems of the so-called "American Hybrid'; and, not least of all, The *Glossator* editors for the assignment, and Nicola Masciandaro and Ryan Dobran for careful and helpful reading and critique.

commentary and a certain kind of illuminating fire in book by claiming that "The poem is throughout a commentary on itself, on culture as revolutionary praxis, on the transcendent still lurking in poetics which attribute to specific poems (or to themselves) the power to illuminate or obscure" (72). It is because of this felicitous confluence of commentarial concerns that this essay, as much as it attempts to review Brady's book, also unfolds as equally concerned with emphasizing and elaborating the problem of fire as a problem of commentary and the question of commentary as a question of fire. As commentary and self-commentary swing infinitely closer to pure autocommentary (the autopoesis of the gloss itself, bracketed, perhaps even without text) this essay will not hesitate, in excess of its capacity as 'review,' to collect notes towards developing a productively enunciated poetics of autocommentary.

Commentary, if it operates like fire, in addition to sharing the capacity for light-production and intentional or unintentional obfuscation from the spread of 'smoke,' would conventionally be thought to need fuel for its combustion: a text. Brady ostensibly begins with texts such as this history of fire elaborated above, and more immediately, her own "verse-essay" as that on which the "commentary on itself" comments. It would seem that "self-commentary" always requires some text which precedes it, and to which it can, in beginning, always refer. But, to be syllogistically crude for the sake of exigency, what if the commentary which in some way *is* fire comments on a text which, in advance, already calls itself fire (and if fire is commentary, already a commentary)? What if the supposedly 'first' text to be glossed is already about a world and a history which seem driven in turn by fire–as Brady puts it, "the globalisation of a fire that feeds on life" (72), again already a collection of a single global gloss–what burns then? Adding up these claims of the book in what seems at first a crudely literal manner points towards the vertiginous limits of commentary appearing somewhere in the neighborhood of 'pure autocommentary'; as flames burning on nothing but flames themselves (the Bachelardian reverie of fire).[2] One might assume that commentary (no matter how much it

[1] See <http://dispatx.com>. I have had consistent trouble accessing the site at the time of the completion of this essay apparently because it seems to be undergoing some kind of reconstruction.

[2] See Gaston Bachelard, *The Poetics of Reverie: Childhood, Language, and the Cosmos*, trans. Daniel Russell (Boston: Beacon, 1969); and *The Psychoanalysis of*

dilates out from the text on which it comments while riding on its own energy) still begins with that prior text on which it comments: a commentary ought to have a text in order to be a commentary and not, say, an essay or a poem or a sacred scripture.

Yet it is the former, more difficult, upshot of the reading of *fire* as a name for a not-necessarily material but certainly substantial and ontological element (or at least elemental principle) of how a world, or a poem, unfolds, that is immediately enacted by the very title of the first section: "Pyrotechne." The neologism insists on fire as a principle of building, or as a principle of how what-is comes to appearance. The second section, similarly, opens by implying fire as elemental to the book's ontology even in advance of its self-commentarial function, as the book slyly announces, in a small stanza set about half-way across the page from the left margin "Remember I am / on fire / cannot be trusted" (13). The book points to itself and claims that the wildfire of its title is literally what it is, points to itself with the fire of commentary and glosses, "Wildfire." At the same time, the line break immediately after only the verb-phrase ("I am / on fire") recalls us to the divine name itself according to Torah as Y--H gives it to Moses, and as God appears in flames which illuminate but do not combust the bush they surround–even as the famously riddling verbal gloss of Y--H (*I am . . . I am that I am*) again slyly

Fire, trans. Alan C.M. Ross (Boston: Beacon 1964). What is most important here is the sense of the comment dreaming of itself, and of its text ahead of the appearance of both of them (text and commentary). When Bachelard asks "if fire, which, after all, is quite an exceptional and rare phenomenon, was taken to be a constituent element of the Universe, is it not because it is an element of human thought, the prime element of reverie," he does so with the confidence that "the dream is stronger than experience" (*Psychoanalysis of Fire*, 18-20). It is by a dialectical process of idealization that Bachelard sees fire and light coincide as love, illumination, annihilation, and thus for Bachelard's spiritualism, life (cf. PF 106). The divine fire, or that of reverie is in contrast as well from fire which appears spontaneous combustion, but is deceptive: "Thus story-tellers, doctors, physicians, novelists, all of them dreamers, start off from the same images and pass on to the same thoughts . . . From the flames which emanate from the *brûlot* they fabricate men of substance. In all cases *attribute values*; they call upon all their own passions to explain a shaft of flame. They put their whole heart into 'communicating' with a spectacle which fills them with wonderment and therefore deceives them" (PF, 98).

obscures the nature and original origin or 'reference' of the flames themselves.[3]

So the question of autocommentary will then hinge on the extent to which Brady's text can consider the possibility of a burning without fuel, something like the pentecostal divine flame of commentary which operates with the structure of divine fire but without the perhaps dangerously gnostic or esoteric element of the divine flame: these would bind commentary to give light to texts in order to produce knowledge about a text as 'salvation' from a flaming world, and which also obfuscates a text for all but the initiate and thus darkens the world–or even leaves it to burn all in its own, caring more for the so-called divine word. Thus Brady seeks the structure of the divine fire without the divinity and its attendant contempt for the world when she recalls a particular story from 1 Kings. She asks, "Was the god talking, or pursuing, / on a journey, or asleep?" (19), recalling a competition between Elijah and four hundred "priests of Baal" to see whose god would call down fire from heaven to consume a sacrifice without a human setting fire to it. The assumption of the competitors is that "the god who answers by fire is indeed god,"[4] and so Elijah taunts the priests by asking if their god was perhaps busy with something more important, like sleep, sex, or even reliving himself, as the priests desperately cut themselves to try to entice their god to perform–before Elijah swiftly soaks his own alter with water (three times for effect) and God sends down fire from heaven which consumes the bull, wood, and even stones of the alter, after which Elijah is authorized to slaughter all four hundred priests of Baal: divine fire's contempt for the world. Still, having exposed the violence which follows the contempt of the divine flames, the poem then commits to entering into this supposedly transcendent fire in the very next line nonetheless, as if to force the hand of its supposed necessity: "The only way out a sea of flames" (19).

Can Brady find–and how will her book look for–a step beyond the self-commentary ("commentary on itself") that she desires for her book: pure autocommentary as fire which, without trying to escape the world into the burning light of gnostic 'salvation,' can burn without combusting a text: pure autocommentary as commentary which comments on nothing but its own comments? This would

[3] Exodus 3, NRSV.
[4] 1 Kings 18:17-40, NRSV.

require flame without fuel–a disturbance in the order of the inevitable, a decidedly worldly turning of flame on itself which, instead of granting respite to the expectation of an otherwordly 'salvation' in 'going up in flames to high heaven' and out of the world,[5] turns in on itself as a way of surprising the orders of necessity in the world without leaving or coming from elsewhere: burning without lightening or darkening–genuine elemental *kinesis*. If fire is a necessity, can the poem go 'down into a burning ring of fire' without burning up itself, disturb what appears as fires inevitable course towards a contemptuous burning of that same world whose appearance fire, as elemental principle, seems to make possible?

ii.

Patient attention to *Wildfire*'s claims about form and relation to form as verse-essay will eventually link Brady's investigation of the inevitable in the history of an elemental/ontological operation of fire to what emerges as not only the problem of, but the need for, autocommentary as a response to the finding oneself amidst such flames. But also–even if only as an aside–such a procedure will help review one way to place the book within more specifically recent work in poetics.

The claim to have written a verse-essay immediately works well with the book's bent to critically interrogate statements which register less as lyrical than philosophical, or even didactic since the 'essay' may at first glance appear an obvious form for such functions. Brady's own recent work and apparent alliances within the current poetry scene would suggest that her readership would be set up to expect a work that is theory-friendly, politically- and philosophically-engaged, and what at least some New York poets might call avant-garde, experimental, or even 'conceptual'–although I do not here

[5] See Paul A. Bové's critique of gnosticism in the humanities, especially as recently exemplified in writing by Slavoj Žižek, in *Poetry Against Torture: Criticism, History, and the Human* (Hong Kong: Hong Kong University Press, 2008): "The new wave of Gnostic or near-Gnostic ambitions, coming after a generation that took seriously the idea that there could be no poetry after Auschwitz, that ruin was inevitable, reflects nothing less than an inability to stand in the face of human self-knowledge stripped of the comforting error of divine infusion. Politics seems unable to redeem time, and so the Christ appears, ready at hand to those with certain kinds of partial memories, ready to comfort us once more" (4-5).

have room to avow or disavow such labels. She is well-known for working between early modern and contemporary poetics as a lecturer at Queen Mary's at the University of London (in which capacity she has published a book on English funerary elegy in the seventeenth century),[6] and directs the "Archive of the Now," which bills itself as "a scholarly, aesthetic, social and political resource for writers and readers of *innovative* poetry" [emphasis mine].[7] Krupsaya, the publisher of *Wildfire* announces on its website that it is "*dedicated* to publishing *experimental* poetry and prose" [italics mine].[8] Brady's past books poetry include *The Rushes, Embrace,* and *Vacation of a Lifetime,* which too hail from presses known for publishing experimental work, like Salt, for example.[9] With Keston Sutherland (whose *White Hot Andy* has been of some importance to the American avant-garde in recent years) Brady also edits Barque Press, which has published distinctly experimental or avant-garde poets including J. H. Prynne, Peter Middleton, and Brian Kim Stefans.

Yet Brady's book resists being innovative or experimental as facile program. Specifically she resists a procedure which sets up a false dilemma between two temporalities or literary genres, pretending they are wildly different or indeed even 'opposites' and mutually exclusive, and then simply mashes them up against each other with the assumption that this is innovation. The mixes of genre and temporality, first of all arriving from historical need and not random pairing in the name of experiment, register as at a level of basic responsibility, as an imperative for a book ambitious enough to take on a problem of global proportions like fire. So *Wildfire*'s willingness to engage so-called 'philosophical discourse' is not only unstinting, but ambitiously turns towards the very dawn of western philosophy in the Heraclitian fragments which Brady renders as

---

[6] Andrea Brady, *English Funerary Elegy in the Seventeenth Century: Laws in Mourning*. (Basingstoke: Palgrave Macmillan, 2006).

[7] Andrea Brady, *Archive of the Now*, "about us," at <http://archiveofthenow.com/about/index.html>, accessed 19 September 2010.

[8] KRUPSKAYA web page, "about us," at <http://krupskayabooks.com/about.htm>, accessed 19 September, 2010.

[9] Andrea Brady, *The Rushes* (Hastings: Reality Street, 2012); *Embrace* (Glasgow: Object Permanence, 2005); *Vacation of a Lifetime* (Cambridge: Salt, 2001).

All things are an equal exchange
for fire and fire for all things,
as goods are for gold and gold for goods . . . (9)

And, more than simply mashing up contemporary poetics and the pre-Socratics, the book allows Heraclitus' fragment to infiltrate the whole of these poetics obsessed with thinking the limits of poetry as liquidating flames.

Certain segments of Brady's readership less disposed to ancient philosophy and expecting what they will want to call innovative or experimental work might be tempted to think of the production of such an essay in verse which includes reference to ancient philosophy as an innovative experiment. But however much we expect to read in justified paragraphs and complete sentences when we encounter either the kind of 'philosophy-writing' from our own era concerned with Heraclitus or critical work under the sign of the 'essay,' we must remember that the pre-Socratic dawn of western philosophy including Heraclitus appeared first to the Greeks in verse in a tradition that would last at least far into the Middle Ages. Along the way to refuting the conception that Parmenides' and Heraclitus' ideas were fundamentally opposed, Martin Heidegger in fact insisted on the importance of poetics to the founding of western philosophical thought.[10] Nor is verse historically foreign to 'scientific' or didactic thought, to which Lucretius' *De Rerum Natura* bears witness. Verse and essay are not even opposites which run into each other at their limits (an idea that will return later in this essay), but are simply compatible forms and modes of a certain poetics of serious historical thought in a tradition which has brought them together whose deep-time (with respect to a human) history makes their employment not innovative or novel, but historical and needful.

Brady not only disavows such facile 'novelty,' she also attempts to demonstrate the imperative for using such a form as part of inhabiting the long tradition she wishes to read in order to look for alternatives within it. Her "Note On the Text" insists on the

[10] Heidegger notes, "The thinking of Parmenides and Heraclitus was still poetic, which in this case means philosophical and not scientific. But because in this poetic thinking the thinking has priority, the thought about man's being follows its own direction and proportions." Martin Heidegger, *An Introduction to Metaphysics*, trans. Ralph Manheim (New Haven: Yale University Press, 1959), 144.

importance of the verse-essay to the ostensible object of inquiry as historical: in "Tracing a globalisation of a fire that feeds on life" (72), as "an interrogation of writing practices that fume as much as they enlighten," and as in fact a "recovery of material history" (71). And, Brady does include a fascinating outward-pointing list of sources, even if they are herded into odd categories that are–in a way at odds with the deft posing of genre in the book's title and body–sometimes historical (Ancient and Early Modern) sometimes 'genre-based' ("Poetic").

Part of the interest of the book for this present journal, however, will appear less in its more restricted claims pertaining to the genre of the 'verse essay' than what appears in Brady's poem as the urgent need to tend not only the poetic aspects of philosophical thought, but their potential–or necessity–for an auto-commentarial surrounding shape, and how the less-desirable aspects of a history of fire and fire-arms ironically make this clear.[11] Thus Brady opens the section of the poem, "Crude," with

> This is automatic fire.
> This is automatic fire, a token ring.
> Each extruder talking English to themselves.
> The technology driven since 4 BCE . . . (45).

The first announcement (*this is automatic fire*) immediately gives way to a second which, in a paratactic but seemingly restrictive clause modifying the complement "automatic fire," comments on it as a "token ring" thus glossing whatever "this" points towards as the very

[11] We can accordingly place *Wildfire* within more recent literary history in noting that for Brady's book the term 'verse-essay' provokes questions on a slightly different trajectory than that of a work like Charles Bernstein's "The Artifice of Absorption." See Bernstein, "The Artifice of Absorption," in *A Poetics* (Cambridge, Mass: Harvard University Press), 9-89. The essay seems to claim itself as both essay and verse by what seems to be a lineation of what is for the most part rather prosaic syntax of the Academic essay as part of the experiment in "artifice." The essay, it should be noted, is of great interest on its own terms as well, and has been formative for a whole generation of an English-speaking poetry avant-garde which has both appropriately and inappropriately imitated and appropriated it. Following the trajectory of its inquiry into form as it regards the 'verse-essay' is by no means prohibitive of following Brady's, and vice-versa.

round structure of a commentary encircling a page in the margins, a ring: "this" is an autocommentary. This sense is furthered by the capacity of a ring of fire or of 'extruders' (are these men or oil mining machines?) to appear equally as the automatic fire of an auto-commentary (an autopoesis? a glossator mining sense from herself or oil from Iraq?) since they are, after all, "talking English to themselves." And yet, that these fragments which hauntingly suggest a *longue durée* history for the M5 rifle also register in a shape and syntactic structure recognized by the student of commentary as the glossed page–this makes equally imperative the need to tend to the auto-consuming of a language and substance of flame in which

> Though the danger of the instability of our weapons
> sometimes results in friendly fire consumption
> of the whole deck, we stick by our strategies,
> or stick like melted candles to the table (50).

And the need for autocommentary on a language that is fire spins out centripetally as well, so that writing as fire must also be understood as commentary on the globe itself, as in this sentence which successfully risks the ostentation of capitalized nouns "Fierce Feavers must calcine the Body of this World" (42). Thus Brady acknowledges the link of the verse-essay as a form to that of commentary as more than simply an attempt to acknowledge some predicable minimum threshold of reflexivity.[12]

The force of Brady's title locates a site where essay and verse coincide in our present historical moment not as a predictable all-too-tired genre-crossing between the supposed difference of poetry and prose, but as authentically emerging in this very particular swoon of at once embracing and rejecting fire as not only a figure for, but also as the literal *ousia* of, a contemporary avant-garde poetry. Specifically because of its relationship to fire, such poetics must also conceive of its task in relation to the world as commentarial even to the extent of becoming auto-commentary. Another way both to figure this problem of the verse-essay in its relation to commentary and fire, and to feel its needfulness in factical historical relation is to recall a moment of Dante's piece of poetics, the *Convivio*, in which the vernacular appears

[12] Regarding Bernstein's essay (see above note), the play of "obscurity and illumination," however, has affinity with that of "artifice" and "absorption"–in both cases each turns into its supposed opposite.

as a kind of poetic prose (a sense perhaps going back to Augustine), or poetics burning within the house of prose (which would of course predate James' house of fiction, and perhaps slide more swiftly into appearing as the house of Being, aflame):

> If flames of fire were seen issuing from the windows of a house, and someone asked if there were a fire within, and another answered in the affirmative, I would not be able to judge easily which of the two was more deserving of ridicule. No different would be the question and answer if someone asked me whether love for my native tongue resides in me and I replied in the affirmative.[13]

Here the vernacular, the house, is aflame with the fires of the poetic tongue in which Dante obviously loves to speak and write (and thus for Dante, that in which he loves to write poems, to love and praise). Needing to point out such obvious love would be ridiculously redundant. And yet, Dante does in fact commit this redundant implied deixis, with the force of an elaborating gloss issuing from the analogy to the burning house. The vernacular, which in and of itself, and in one's love for it, apparently needs no gloss (unlike, of course, a supposedly global high and poetic language, a language of scripture which demands exegesis) and yet cannot help but glossing itself, even when it is most aware of the supposed redundancy. The verse-essay, similarly a vernacular sort of poetics, verging on the didactic, redundantly needs no gloss and yet somehow, on close inspection, might consist only in glossing itself.

While all the whole of the above citation of Dante is here helpful, what is perhaps most important for the moment is again the historical force it brings down upon the exigencies of Brady's form as it consistently links the history of the thought-attempt (or essay) in verse both with commentary and with fire. More succinctly: what I want to praise about Brady's book depends a great deal on the possibility that a verse-essay would be possible at this moment to the extent that poetry at once is elementally fire and the escape (as water, or what element?) from the inevitability of fire as total

---

[13] Dante Alighieri, *Convivio*, trans. Richard Lansing, in *Digital Dante* on the Columbia University Website, Book 1, Ch. 12, accessed at <http://dante.ilt.columbia.edu/books/convivi/convivio.html> on 19 September 2010. Thanks to Nicola Masciandaro for the reference.

exchangeability, and the extent that, realizing this, it accepts what Derrida once called "the necessity of commentary."[14] Throughout our questions will have to ask if autocommentary helps with the problem of exegesis as a flame which illuminates a text on the condition that it, at the same time, pass into its opposite and obscure the World.

And these lines from *Wildfire* already quoted which seem to veer towards autocommentary also seem to form part of a notable rhythm which moves refreshingly between complete sentences–whether cited, parodied, or moving towards something like 'direct philosophical statement'–and the kind of disjunctive syntax which avoids certain traps of boredom and lost energy, thus negotiating this problem of supposed oppositions. While brilliant, challenging, and necessary in its L=A=N=G=U=A=G=E incarnations such as Silliman's sentences, Clark Coolidge's strings of broken self reference (e.g. *At Egypt*) or Bernadette Mayer's broken and constantly re-breaking recursivity,[15] such practices are all-to-often appropriated not as innovative composition but as depraved calculation resulting in a canned "disjunctive syntax" that easily becomes either a crutch for an avant-garde (for those times it remains unwilling to truly dismantle lyricism and/or simply lacking the commitment to maintain the energy or patience and a critical thought beyond the span of a string of two or three words), or, alternately, an easy excuse for the now Norton-anthologized 'American Hybrid' whose proponents, again, in depraved calculation, would like to believe that *lyric + disjunctive syntax = redemption of lyric.*[16] But Brady's verse works hard to offer alternatives to such dead-ends without running back into the safety of the prosaic. For that would merely consist of one of the obvious

[14] Cf. Jacques Derrida, "Edmond Jabès and the Question of the Book," in *Writing and Difference*, trans. Alan Bass (Chicago: University of Chicago Press, 1978), 67.

[15] See especially Mayer's and Coolidge's sentences going productively clashing with and cross-infecting each other in the only recently published collaboration (although written long previous) *The Cave* (Michigan: Adventures in Poetry, 2009).

[16] See Jeff T. Johnson's recent review "The New Hybridity: *Bird Lovers, Backyard* by Thalia Field and *Floats Horse-floats or Horse-flows* by Leslie Scalapino," in *Fanzine,* 6 September 2010, on *thefanzine.com* accessed at <http://thefanzine.com/articles/books/461/the_new_hybridity_bird_lovers,_backyard_by_thalia_field_and_floats_horse-floats_or_horse-flows_by_leslie_scalapino>, 9 September, 2010.

manifestations of fire and commentary as mutually problematic by which Brady is deeply troubled: the conversion of one thing into its opposite through some common element, what the very syntax of lines such as these both point to and resist at the pole of 'the complete sentence':

> Anything organic can be drawn, calcined
> for days on the stove, from this need for gold. (24)

But these lines are gloss and are glossed by, on the very next page, a syntax that breaks roughly mid-line and across enjambments, sloughing together strings of logic via the poetic metonymy of the page and not the math-logic prosaic syntax:

> Is this labour, pinks
> unfading perennials, tarnish its aim:
> by return to uncover what in the composition–
> that nothing turns on illumination . . . (25)

Here is the syntax which just for a brief moment might appear, given its confusion of which words operate as verbs and which as nouns, which seems to lack a subject, which conjures the specters of L=A=N=G=U=A=G=E-schooled verse à la Clark Coolidge, Lyn Hejinian, or Barrett Watten, or at very least their late-sixties predecessors. Trying all its joints in the syntax of a question which breaks off without resolving in an up-intonation of the question-mark, the verse itself becomes the object of its deixis (*Is this*). And this turn to point back at itself is notable not only because we do not know what exactly is calling attention to itself, but also because this pointing is elaborative: these verbs of alternating conjugations (*pinks*, sg. present tense; *tarnish*, pl. present tense) elaborate a sort of olfactory surface (giving us whiffs of color and chemical reaction, oxidation, without telling us exactly how they register) while they wrap about we know not what subject–save the one around which they swirl in elaboration –as *autocommentary*.

iii.

Brady's "Note On the Text" additionally states (in terms which acknowledge the ambition of such a statement)[17] that her book attempts "to persuade us, to recognize that certain catastrophes and felicities are not inevitable" and that "It concerns the history of incendiary devices, of the evolution of Greek fire from a divine secret which could sustain or destroy empires, into white phosphorus and napalm; the elliptical fires or the pre-Socratics . . . " (71). Such a pronouncement accounts for what a reader quickly recognizes as the book's attempt to constantly register disquiet at the extent to which it finds a certain lay reading of the debates of the pre-Socratics sadly *adequate* to representing the problem of writing as illumination in a world where it is flaming oil fields which give light to the scholar headed for Mesopotamia's plundered museums, and writing itself is an instrument of enlightenment only insofar as it allows the world to be obscured by the smoke from incendiary precision bombing or the screens of secret prisons: "But for the apocalypse they give us freedom / of information act, and for 2d five sparrows: that nothing / concealed will not be revealed" (57). That is, the book wants to resist a state of affairs in which the pronouncement that change and motion are impossible is an adequate assumption when describing the history in which "the irenic languages of love, philosophy, and poetry are so indebted to fire; why we burn, melt, smoulder, are pierced with burning arrows from flaming eyes and in repose are lit by the light of nature" (72)—and the book wants to wrestle with the knowledge that poetry tends to fan these flames as from them it borrows its very substance.

The virtue of Brady's book is in its willingness consider, at very least thematically, the extent to which the auto-commentarial might head off the burns of obscurity and illumination as some kind of authentic movement, a way of trying to—as John D. Caputo puts it in his *Radical Hermeneutics*—"read the *kinesis* back into *ousia*, to read *ousia*

[17] Brady's notes on the text indicate that she in fact had attempted to write about war in Iraq and *Gilgamesh* in which "Epic fragments were transported by Penguin Classics to a nook in London then back out to a pixillated field sewn with cluster bomblets and the shards of the Nemean lion." She then admits, "Although its aims are equally immodest, *Wildfire* was somehow more possible to stick to" (72).

back down into its kinetic components."[18] Brady strikes out for the margins with words that confuse what is at stake as a way of raising the stakes.

> Light is everything, is the opposite of fat, is relish
> without coping
>
> Law promethean, expectation
> bound not binding. (56)

Is this light the problem of the burning of human bodies, or a ridiculous revision of the Presocratic debates about the elements (adding lipids to the usual earth, fire, water, etc.), or is it the problem of *relish*, of enjoyment itself, now reframed as a plume of oily smoke from flesh? Does this "relish/ without coping" register the hope of shaking-up a cosmos built on fire? What is that which is 'bound but not binding,' that light adds to our bodies only as burnability, as mere savory relish to the brazier of human existence? That it is in fact 'relish,' but without 'coping,' is exactly what makes her text a movement towards motion, and what makes it commentarial.

Remembering that a text is bound but not binding, as well as reading the word 'relish' may remind of Nicola Masciandaro's claim, in his manifesto concerning the spiciness of commentary as geophilosophy, that

> commentary, which happens in proximity to and not (as in the case of its bastard offspring the annotated critical edition) in parenthesis from the text, which moves from this proximity as the very ground of its truth, and which is saturated with its own event in the form of the *extra* or outside presence of its essentially deictic gesture, may be called the *savoury circulation of the interruption of our exposure to the otherwise.*[19]

The commentarial, after all, follows the text as if a law in an inevitable course while not following the necessary path, striking

[18] John D. Caputo, *Radical Hermeneutics: Repetition, Deconstruction, and the Hermeneutic Project* (Bloomington: Indiana University Press, 1987), 1-3.
[19] Nicola Masciandaro, "Becoming Spice: Commentary as Geophilosophy," *Collapse VI: Geo/Philosophy* (2010): 48.

digressively out to the margins even as it is bound to stay with the text, bulking up the volume as it goes along. For, when one asks of her own poem "How long can this long / advert get through / a history in which all events are the same? (7), in a time when a certain debased version of negative critique in the Academic discourse *can* appear dangerously indulgent or intoxicating, when, "Now / negation is so sweetly irresistible" (68), a movement toward something 'extra' is needed–a movement that commits no flight to transcendence but maintains the inevitable path in the shape of the World of finite beings even as it works to unravel inevitability and necessity. A hip performative metaphoricity added to a negative critique would not more exempt it from the problem–one is merely burning up:

> And if I were to use that language–a mode
> that absorbs its screening mass from the atmosphere
> of commerce, politics and waste, from the family . . .
>
> . . . have I scored a blinder, or run blind
> myself in all this vapour quickly spending
> its burn I think I'm seeing the future? (51)

Neither 'workshop' craft nor canned disjunctive syntax applied to a current global concern can simply be added as if in a chemical formula to yield any authentic *change*–the accidental aesthetics of bygone experimental or avant-garde poetry too easily pass through fire and into their opposites. Unexamined 'oppositional' form as well will only provide more fuel for what burns up all the world so that the inevitability of war is reinforced. This is why throughout the text Brady echoes Nietzsche's musings on a *Chemistry of concepts and sensations* in which

> At almost every point, philosophical problems are once again assuming the same form for the questions as they did two thousand years ago: how can something arise from its opposite, for example something rational from something irrational, something sentient from something dead, logic

> from illogic, disinterested contemplation from willful desire, living for others from egoism, truth from error?[20]

Brady writes:

> Clearance of one organisation to its opposite
> is known as no man's
> land is all the difference
> between loyalty and hate (50)

and then underscores that "the logic of elemental opposition has reached its end" (50)–that in some cases illicit mutual complicity of phenomena no longer bothers to even appear in terms of opposites in order to mask its non-movement with façade of authentic change. This is why *Wildfire* desires a movement out towards the margins for something 'extra' as commentary, but attempts this in a turning inward on itself (autocommentary: looking for its marginalia within itself), a stirring capable of disturbing: a stirring within itself as a stirring up of a movement, a shake-up as a something 'extra,' and a stirring-*in* the extra 'spice' of commentary. In this turning-in what gets added is a movement: a *kinesis* in/as the *ousia* of poesis, as the poesis of the autocommentarial. Such is one way this piece realizes this mode, just as the positions in the book of the question referred to above beginning "How can this long / advert get through" and the statement that "Negation is sweetly irresistible" might be reversed, as if the early question which would seem to demand some kind of alternative is the gloss, laid up in advance, on the self-indicting comment which comes at the end–a self-enfolding movement whose flip and fold we hope generates a ripple in the stream of the same. In fact, upon re-reading, Brady's claim that the text comments on itself is realized, whether or not in compositional technique, at least in the experience of finding the entire contents of her book as miraculously 'extra' without letting us for a second have an answer to the question 'extra to what?'

---

[20] Friedrich Nietzsche, *Human, All Too Human*, vol. 1, *The Complete Works of Friedrich Nietzsche*, trans. Gary Handwerk (Stanford: Stanford University Press, 1997), 3. 15-16.

iv.

More of the ambition of *Wildfire*:

> the poem stems from a desire to counter legal and extra-legal violence not with the naive pacifism that demands only (only?) ban to the worst weapons or the end of all war–but with an understanding of our deep affections for fire, fires that consume, obliterate, stick and burn clear, that transform, catch, and outshine. (73)

To do this, Brady is even willing to risk the Eliotic attempt to move towards poetry as direct philosophical statement, but without telling us exactly what she's philosophizing about, so that the effect, again, is an attempt at a necessary superfluity as an alternative to burnability: a desperate attempt to produce something that will leave a residue once the flames have subsided, and yet without the sense that what is to be added might come from elsewhere. What is extra must somehow get produced from within the curve of the World and the Finite, such as here, with the combustion of the human body:

> With the powder dry references scatter,
> but we began with somewhat that belonged
> to the body of man . . . (38)

But since such residue only comes *after* violent death, and since we recall that the problem of fire remains *global*, such violence cannot help get at, from the very start, what is extraneous.

So where does one begin? Perhaps the clearest exposition that one aim of Brady's book consists of a hope that the commentarial path of circumnavigation–a rehearsal of the same folding in on itself–might generate some alternatives are these lines found early in the poem:

> I have tried to make in a month what the sun
> accomplishes in a year as in the brass sphere,
> an excess, believing
>
> if in fire we are in our element
> then something can displace us,

> that the hope is in
> the recitation
>
> I might find not fire
> but thick water (10)

Yet in this formulation of autocommentarial poetics as a desire for an 'extra' resulting from movement, Brady here stumbled on the above-noted difficulty to which Derrida refers in writing of Edmond Jabès:

> The necessity of commentary, like poetic necessity, is the very form of exiled speech. In the beginning is hermeneutics. But the *shared* necessity of exegesis, the interpretive imperative, is interpreted differently by the rabbi and the poet. The difference between the horizon of the original text and exegetic writing makes the difference between the rabbi and the poet irreducible. Forever unable to reunite with each other, yet so close to each other, how could they ever regain the *realm*?[21]

Among those confronted above, a difficulty in claiming an autocommenterial poetics in a poem which both recognizes and rejects the notion that everything is, so to speak, for fire equally exchangeable and understands the challenge of facing the Same, is that such a commentary might begin or end anywhere.

It is a problem of ignition. Where, after all would a poem have to begin to consist entirely of pure autocommentary? What words could the poet start writing? This is perhaps an unfair question to take this poem to task for, but one the poem to its credit, provokes. Autocommentarial verse-essay as a poem about nothing thus takes on everything and anything, and, paradoxically, remains very specific. A final digressive comment borrowing once again from philosophy will be necessary for this oddly long review to even begin to consider how to ask a question about this problem.

We could easily say this book begins, if anywhere, on no ground other than a certain kind of ambition, such as at the head of

[21] Derrida, "Edmond Jabès and the Question of the Book," in *Writing and Difference*,67.

the section titled "Love's Fire," where the very title takes part in this motion, as well as its first lines:

> Smothered in bitter wine or mud, heart's fire
> your moist air *immo fomento alitur umberrimo*
> an altogether different poison revised with kerosene
> that enlightens the closed garden where she sits. (61).

Even with the word "kerosene" which literalizes the 'burning' of "heart's fire," these lines risk indictment not only for alluding to whole histories of conventional and canned love-poetry, but also for their critique of it in terms no less obvious than echoes of that room in Eliot's *Waste Land* in which the "flames of the sevenbranched candelabra" are reflected in a depiction of the rape of Philomel on the wall (foretelling the ugly yet tepid rape of the woman in the next section of the poem).[22] But the attempt of the verse, its essay-quality, *is* thus its own self assertion. It consists in this willingness to attempt to produce a poem without washing one's hands of the world, or the possibility of writing a 'bad' poem. Even if the material means of production are peeled back by pointing out the chemical source of the flames of love in a gas lamp in this particular garden, and this is opposed to the conventional relationship of fire and love in western verse, the effect of leading with "bitter wine" is irreversible: nothing says "I am a poem" to a lay-reader more than wine or fire, no matter what context is revealed in close reading. Such ambition declares the assertion of a poem, of ambition itself, by beginning with an assertion

[22] See T.S. Eliot, *The Waste Land,* in *Collected Poems 1909-1962* (NY: Harcourt, 1963), p. 56, lines 77-93, The scene takes up the bulk of part II, "A Game of Chess," and is worth recalling more fully as an important point of reflection and pervasive allusion (along with Eliot in general) of *Wildfire*: "The Chair she sat in, like a burnished throne, / Glowed on the marble, where the glass / Held up by standards wrought with fruited vines / From which a golden Cupidon peeped out / (Another his eyes behind his wing) / Doubled the flamed of the sevenbranched candelabra / Reflecting the light upon the table as / The glitter of her jewels arose to meet it, / From satin cases poured in rich profusion. / In vials of ivory and coloured glass / Unstoppered, lurked her strange synthetic perfumes, / Unguent, powdered, or liquid-troubled, confused / And drowned the sense in odours; stirred by the air / That freshened from the window, these ascended / In fattening the prolonged cangle-flames, / Flung their smoke into the laquearia, / Stirring the pattern on the coffered ceiling."

that doubles as a gloss, both which read, "this is a poem." Yet even here, there is only the ash of a failed poetic idiom to assert, the autocommentary could not have arisen from anything. Eliotic fire is thus deeply troubling to and troubled by Brady's book, and indeed in this light her rendering of Heraclitus cited above (*All things are an equal exchange/ for fire*) is equally filtered and colored by Eliot's "death of fire,"[23] and equally concerned with the apparent no-where out of which a first-spark seems to appear. It may seem that the autocommentarial, as the commentarial capacity of Brady's poem would begin with some prior substance (the text of the 'verse-essay, for instance), unless, again we rigorously and very literally take and temporalize *auto*commentary as not just what automatically comments on itself, but what appears at once as only comment as such with only itself as comment for a text. Before it begins, pure autocommentary at its limit has nothing to comment on.

Autocommentarial verse would consist in just this ambition of making a move to turning-in-on-itself when there is nothing in particular there yet (*pace* Rilke, "Be–and yet know the great *void* where all things begin, / the infinite *source* of your own more intense vibration" [italics mine]).[24] This first turning-in is thus turned-in in a

---

[23] You know the lines, both those concerning how "Water and fire succeed / The town, the pasture and the weed. / Water and fire deride / The sacrifice that we denied. / Water and fire shall rot / The marred foundations we forgot, / Of Sanctuary and choir. / This is the death of water and fire," and those lines in which "The dove descending breaks the air / With flame of incandescent terror . . . The only hope, or else despair / Lies in the choice of pyre or pyre– / To be redeemed from fire by fire." See Eliot, *Collected Poems* 1909-1962, p.202 & 207. Moreover of course the final Dantean lines of the *Quartets* are here worth noting, in which "All shall be well" when among other things, "the fire and the rose are one." These lines on their own demonstrate the spirit/letter, pattern/execution, form/content, and commentary/text relationship in a particular figure Eliot intends to be complicit in his (mis)claiming of Julian of Norwich's "all shall be well" (Julian's own self-commentary on her autommentarial vision). See pp. 208-209.

[24] See Rainier Maria Rilke, "Sonnets to Orpheus," Part 2, XIII, in *Ahead of All Parting: Poetry and Prose of Rainer Maria Rilke*, ed. and trans. Stephen Mitchell (NY: Modern Library, 1995), 487 (Ger. text 486):

> Be ahead of all parting, as though it already were
> behind you, like the winter that has just gone by.
> for among these winters there is one so endlessly winter
> that only by wintering through it will your heart survive.

direction towards whatever (absolutely anything) as well as toward the nothing itself that the auto-commentary remains with nothing yet to double back on. The feeling of reading Brady's book is of a constant veer towards the limit of auto-commentary, no matter how much she may theoretically have the 'text' of the verse-essay as supposedly separate from its movement of self-commentary to comment begin with. Although Brady's book deals with a very material history it would seem both that the relation of what consists of a 'material' for writing appears more in this movement around the surface of a we-know-not-what than an assumption of a classical understanding of *ousia* simply as empirically discoverable and shapable 'substance.' A commitment to this sort of commentary–to orbit what may after all be only other orbits disturbing obits–appears as a best hope in the search for alternatives to that divine fire which flames up in contempt of the world and indeed the material whose materiality that same burning ironically attempts to secure via the "transcendence still lurking in poetics which attribute to specific poems (or to themselves) the power to illuminate or obscure"–a transcendence which is, as noted above, such a deeply troubling phenomenon to Brady and indeed a purported occasion for the book (72).

To the extent the book veers towards pure autocommentary–miraculously non-combusting flames surrounding miraculously non-combusting flame, a read feels very much in the swirl of this problem of genesis. This is a ~~moment~~ where commentary stands in as a paradigm of the problem of genesis in all writing, when it could be 'about' anything or everything, but remains forever nothing–cannot in fact begin. Again, commentary is conventionally about something,

---

Be forever dead in Eurydice–more gladly arise
into the seamless life proclaimed in your song.
here, in the realm of decline, among momentary days,
be the crystal cup that shattered even as it rang.

Be–and yet know the great void where all things begin,
the infinite source of your own more intense vibration,
so that, this once, you may give it your perfect assent.

To all that is used-up, and to all the muffled and dumb
creatures in the world's full reserve, the unsayable sums,
joyfully as your*self*, and cancel the count.

conventionally comments on a text and maintains a kind of expanding specificity. To return to Masciandaro:

> Infinite commentary on an infinitesimal text is commentary's ideal, not actually, but only as an unimaginable concept reasserting its deep desire, namely, to spatially achieve the ontological breaking-point of the text, the situation where there is *neither anything outside the text nor nothing outside the text.*[25]

So for the limit phenomenon of pure autocommentary, a text that begins by referring to itself, to begin, is in Derridean parlance, always already a *renvoi* (re-sending), marked by an *a priori* divisibility that is for all that not a lack or negativity: "Everything begins by referring back [*par le renvoi*], that is to say does not begin."[26] In this respect, what one might detect as a persistent obsession with embodiment and its relation to fire (fats, ashes, etc.) in *Wildfire* is fortuitous. Such poesis

---

[25] Masciandaro, "Becoming Spice," 54.

[26] See "Envoi," trans. Peter and Mary Ann Caws, in *Psyche: Inventions of the Other* Vol. 1: "Everything begins by referring back [*par le renvoi*], that is to say does not begin. Given that this effraction or this partition divides every *renvoi* from the start, there is not a single *renvoi* but from then on, always, a multiplicity of *renvois*, so many different traces referring back to other traces and to traces of others. This divisibility of the envoi has nothing negative about it, it is not a lack, it is altogether different from subject, signifier, or the letter that Lacan says does not tolerate participation and always arrives as destination. This divisibility of difference is the condition for there being any envoi, possibly and envoi of Being, a dispensation or a gift of being and time, of the present and of representation . . . As soon as there are *renvois*, and they are always already there, something like representation no longer waits and one must perhaps make do with that so as to tell oneself this story otherwise, from *renvois* to *renvois* of *renvois*, in a destiny that is never guaranteed to gather itself up, identify itself, or determine itself. I do not know if this can be said with or without Heidegger, and it does not matter. This is the only chance–but it is only a chance for there to be history, meaning, presence, truth, language, theme, thesis, and colloquium." Thus Derrida hope for something related to "the unrepresentable, not only as that which is foreign to the very structure of representation, as what one *cannot* represent, but rather and also what one *must not* represent, whether or not it had the structure of the representable . . . the immense problem of the *prohibition* that beat on representation . . . " (126-128). With respect to the problem of thinking the genesis of autocommentary, I refer to all the same structures.

could not *begin* but would have to emerge as a *body* which is a movement of a boundary (the marginal sphere of commentary) around a nothing in such a way that this nothing remained open to the outside. Alternately, as a body, autocommentary would appear, whole, fleshly, by referring to its own auto-replicating genetic code (as certain kind of asexual reproductive model). It must at once take up space and be flat, be plural *and* monadic without being merely plural. Autocommentary would be the bringing into the world of something new in which text must be encountered as body, recalling Gérard Granel's assertion (which echoes Derrida's comments on the *renvoi* above) that "The body is the site of diversification of the a priori of the visible. It is the pure ontological site"[27]–thus the problem of being able to talk about anything but having to begin seemingly as nothing.

Reading a line of *Wildfire* as a layer of skin on such a body would be to mark Brady's poem, at a moment when much of the so-called avant-garde is content to pay attention to mere quirkiness in the hope of raising an interesting issue accidentally or along the way as a side-effect (a kind of poetics as pharmaceutical R&D investment whose profit depends on stumbling upon off-label uses), with a refreshing ambition which gives relish without coping (without pretending to resolve the world by returning itself to itself, but returning itself to itself in such a way that a ripple of disturbance skids across the curved surface of cosmological happening). Such ambition to write an 'important' poem curves flat space into the planetary or global space which Nicola Masciandaro points to as the very spherical movement of commentary–surrounding even in its moment of deixis:

> Accordingly, commentary works to hold forever open *and* totally fill writing's space, as if to absolutely disclose the place of writing, which means to realize it as *curved space*, the immanent space-becoming-place through which everything leads back to itself. This spatial curving that commentary realizes is visible materially as the becoming-round of the text/commentary border and conceptually as the turning motion commentarial reading and writing take:

---

[27] Gérard Granel, "Far From Substance: Whither and to What Point?" translated and reprinted as an appendix in Jean-Luc Nancy, *Dis-Enclosure: The Deconstruction of Christianity*, trans. Bettina Bergo, Gabriel Malenfant, and Michael B. Smith (see note 17) (NY: Fordham, 2008), 173.

> away from the text, turning back towards it, repeat . . . Commentary rotationally transforms the *space* of writing into an earthly *place*. Simple textual space-filling discloses the space of writing as writing's potentiality, the page, by enclosing and surrounding it *from the inside*. Commentary, whose meaning is founded upon proximate separation from its text, continues the enclosure *from within the outside* and thus holds open the space of writing by bounding it, pushes writing to the limit where the space of writing *intersects* with what it already is, the real space of the world.[28]

Autocommentary is a texturing of nothing into a body which can move through the world and disturb whatever moves through its curved lens-like space-time. Thus while Masciandaro is right that commentary forms the sphere where everything leads back to itself, it leads in such a way that exerts a gravitational pull which disrupts and disturbs each and every vector of force which holds the globe (or infinitesimal globule) together (including even those lines of force returning to themselves). Such commentary as the principle of the globe's self-disruption is not unlike the cartographic gloss: mapmaking as the dis-ordering elaboration of the globe's surface which renders it variously as Worlds.

The implicit claims to what is at stake in *Wildfire* as its politics–even beyond the obvious concerns of militarized burn of the globe–is the way a commentarial texturing/elaboration of nothing can paradoxically come to form the becoming of a poem: that in which what comes to be does indeed come to appearance, an *ousia* that is nothing at all (yet without being a lack or a negativity).[29] The claim is

[28] Masciandaro, "Becoming Spice," 54.

[29] With Derrida, I suspect that try as we may, it may be impossible to escape the critique of the determination of Being as Presence. But if the sense of *ousia* as the texturing or elaboration (as self-stirring, as *kinesis*) of nothing at all can be even *implied* (much less ever *found, relied on*, or *proved*), then I do think one can uncover a very different sort of *ousia* than that in the most metaphysical of cosmologies: one characterized by authentic movement which would ripple the fabric of World, an *ousia* (recalling the phrase in Granel's title cited above in note 17) "far from substance." At very least it would revise what one would mean to think about in reading Heidegger's more explicit statements on the term, even in his *Introduction to Metaphysics*, where one must

that a poem is a body that is bound, but only by its unboundedness to the world rushing in on it, unable to stem that flow of leaves, shirts, guns, organs, nymphs, and even margins filling up its margins:

> This point is not being finished with writing, but writing's becoming an unending beginning, the sphericization of the space of writing or our finding of the page as *unbounded finitude*, a surface for limitless writing whose every mark is first and last. Commentary's filling of the margins is an exercise in intentional, exuberant futility directed toward an ultimate forgetting of the outside, toward continual

---

unabashedly confront both metaphysics and their complicity in reprehensible politics. At the moment Heidegger explicitly defines Being as presence, *presence*–though still subject to Derrida's critique–appears differently than one might expect: "But from an observer's point of view, what stands-there-in-itself becomes what puts itself forth, what offers itself in how it looks. The Greeks call the look of a thing its *eidos* or idea . . . What grounds and holds together all the determinations of Being we have listed is what the Greeks experienced without question as the meaning of Being, which they called *ousia*, or more fully, *parousia*. The usual thoughtlessness translates *ousia* as 'substance' and thereby misses its sense entirely. In German, we have an appropriate expression for *parousia* in our word *An-wesen* <coming-to-presence>. We use *Anwesen* as a name for a self-contained farm or homestead. In Aristotle's times, too, *ousia* was still used in this sense *as well as* in its meaning as a basic philosophical word. Something comes to presence. It stands in itself and thus puts itself forth. It is. For the Greeks, 'Being,' fundamentally means presence" (66-67). *Ousia* will emerge in terms of movement, leaving its meaning as what comes to presence very different than if substantiality is understood in terms of physical 'matter' (as defined by empirical science). When *phusis* as *sway* thus comes to stand in/as Being (a horizontal movement), the holding against and with which this emerges (*ousia*) is constancy in a way very different than one might think despite being a "constantly"–for it is by no means a stillness. And this is already in Heidegger, for whom the constancy of Being is said in *phusis* as "arising and standing forth" and in *ousia* in a way that *is* "'constantly,' that is, enduringly, abiding" in which what is *constantly* coming to be does so in which what can only be called constant struggle (*polemos*) (cf. 65). Given its relation to *polemos*, that which is "that within which it becomes" (69) is actually less like the "sway, rest and movement" which are "closed and opened up from an originary unity" (which sounds just so *still* for the sense of a *phusis* constantly self-arising "and within which *that which* comes to presence essentially unfolds as beings" (64)) than it is to an originary *kinesis*. What we call substance might be the movement of nothing.

> writing of the omnipresent impossibility of separateness, the always-never asymptotic union of text and world.[30]

Such poetics could only appear as such thanks to a hidden and exiled ontology, since it would have to look something like what, with reference to Granel, Jean-Luc Nancy has called "the simultaneity of the open and the ringed, the bordered, the cerned or the dis-cerned, and the simultaneity of the void and the divided out."[31] When even the avant-garde disavows ambition of any kind, even for their work, and turns itself to worry about anything other than cosmology (and especially about its academic status), this reviewer would not bother to make pretense to judge the effectiveness of this attempt to produce a spark under erasure, but merely recommend that readers stay, in the spirit of commentary, along the paths of its weird contours. Poems as ambitious embodiment are so refreshing at the moment that adjudicating their success is neither here nor there, as long as a poets would once again care to interfere in philosophy, and not give up on that discourse–so it is a young poet and not just Jean-Luc Nancy (for whom I have nonetheless nothing but respect and admiration) who will ask "How do we touch, or let ourselves be touched by, the opening of the world / to the world?"[32] Brady's book may help along these lines if we try to learn from its attempt to change terms from heat and light to mass and gravity; from what we know and can circulate, to what falls, and even for a moment, stays.

---

[30] Masciandaro, "Becoming Spice," 55.
[31] Jean-Luc Nancy, "A Faith that is Nothing at All," trans. Bettina Bergo, in *Dis-Enclosure: The Deconstruction of Christianity* (New York: Fordham, 2008), 73.
[32] Ibid., 73.

Daniel C. Remein holds an MFA in poetry from the University of Pittsburgh and is a Ph.D. student at New York University in English. His piece "new work: a prosimetrum" appeared in the first issue of *Glossator,* and he has an essay forthcoming in *Postmedieval: A Journal of Medieval Cultural Studies.* Other forthcoming work includes a chapter co-written with Anna Kłosowska, "What Does Language Speak? Feeling the Human with Samuel Beckett and Chrétien de Troyes," for a volume of collected essays from OSU press titled *Fragments for a History of A Vanishing Humanism.* His poems have appeared in numerous journals including *Sentence*, *Sidebrow*, and *LIT.* Remein is a member of the BABEL working group, the founding editor of the literary journal *Whiskey & Fox,* and a co-founder of the Organism for Poetic Research along with its publication *Pelt.*

dESIRE Gloss: A Specimen

Kristen Alvanson, Nicola Masciandaro & Scott Wilson

Presented here is a specimen of *dESIRE Gloss*, a collaborative commentary on a series of 100 photographs drawn from Kristen Alvanson's *dESIRE Project*.[1] Befitting the polysemy of the word *gloss*,

[1] "THE DESIRE PROJECT is an ongoing investigation on dESIRE which includes artistic components, the anti-disciplinary reading of desire texts by individuals such as Deleuze and Guattari, Foucault, Baudrillard, Lyotard, Melanie Klein, Reich, Marx, Freud, de Sade, Irigaray, Hegel, Bataille, Sartre, Derrida, Barthes, Levinas, Plato, Augustine–from which thoughts and theories are disjointed, re-assembled, blended, ruled out–and conversations on dESIRE with current theorists and artists or other desire-minded individuals all in an attempt to reach concrete but not necessarily corporeal definitions of dESIRE by tapping into its obscure formations. CAPTURING dESIRE. Is it possible to capture desire whether abstractly, sensationally or concretely? Is it possible that an event or an entity is desired? Do we have any control over our desires or are they desiring-machines, flows as Deleuze and Guattari suggest? Are we aware of our desires consciously or do they operate according to another plane hidden or not directly connected to consciousness? To further these and other questions, I have developed an experiment as an art project which involves capturing what I desire on a long-term basis. HOW THE PROJECT WORKS. When I desire something, I document the dESIRE by capturing its photograph (currently using a compact camera that I carry wherever I go). Presumably, the photograph is a photographic representation of my intangible desire, yet it serves as a form of documentation. Each stamped (or numbered dESIRE) is a part of the ongoing string of desires which should reveal patterns which are not necessarily visual or thematic over time. I am as interested in the intangible desire and its qualities as I am interested in the photographic renderings – how, for example, a photo reveals accurately or inaccurately an intangible desire. Moreover, I am engaging in marketing and selling my dESIRES, both intangible and photographic representations. What are the potentialities and effects of selling desire and how can pimping dESIRE be used to better understand and test the economy and dynamics of desire? Once desires are produced, represented, sold, purchased and possessed, the dESIRE Project

dESIRE Gloss is designed to demonstrate the amorous relations between photography, commentary, and desire.

*

003580

WINGS OF DESIRE. "The children of men take refuge in the shadow of thy wings. / They feast on the abundance of thy house, / and thou givest them drink from the river of thy delights. / For with thee is the fountain of life; and in thy light do we see light."[2] Do not ask

IN SACRIFICE, beauty's perfection points to death's full brutality. Double-take. At first glance, it is as if the veiled woman is warding off the camera, the hennaed hands not so much a blessing as a curse. But it is the backs of her hands that are visible, of course,

will be also a speculation on Intangible or Immaterial Art" (<http://kristenalvanson.com/new/about.html>. Further documentation, including the artist's essay "The Art of Nothing: Immateriality and Intangible Art," is available on the website.

[2] Psalm 36:7-9, *The New Oxford Annotated Bible* (New York: Oxford University Press, 1977).

about this desire–"Love's pain, I have endured to such a degree–that ask not. / Separation's poison, I have tasted in such a way–that ask not"[3]–about what is clear–"Beauty [*claritas, splendor formae*] re-spects the cognitive power, for things which please in being seen are called beautiful"[4]–about what comes seminally with its own commentary–"all our so-called consciousness is a more or less fantastic commentary on an unknown, perhaps unknowable, but felt text"[5]–about what I cannot not *gloss*: "the phantasm generates desire, desire is translated into words, and the word defines a space wherein the appropriation of what could otherwise not be appropriated or enjoyed is possible."[6] There is no answer, only translation, repetition of the question. That is enough, everything. For it is splayed out and thrust towards the camera lens in pride and supplication, the tattoos perhaps signifying a forthcoming marriage. But then again, these hands are so much in the foreground that they are positioned in the picture almost as if they were 'our' hands–or indeed the photographer's hands that should be taking the photo. It is as if we have suddenly dropped our camera in order to hold back some sinister apparition looming up from behind the glass. The blurring of the picture gives, for me, this sense of double movement, pushing back and forward, thrusting and repelling. A woman beautified, ceremonially painted-up, adorned, veiled for someone's delight, looks ominous. 'We', similarly adorned, *hold back*, with our

---

3 Hafiz of Shiraz, *The Divan*, tr. H. Wilberforce Clarke (London: Octagon Press, 1974), 313.1.

4 "Pulchrum autem respicit vim cognoscitivam, pulchra enim dicuntur quae visa placent" (Aquinas, *Summa Theologiae*, I.5.4), < http://www.corpusthomisticum.org/sth1003.html>.

5 Friedrich Nietzsche, *Daybreak: Thoughts on the Prejudices of Morality*, eds. Maudemaire Clark and Brian Leiter (Cambridge: Cambridge University Press, 1997), 2.119. Whence philosophy as essentially the *practice* of consciousness. Cf. "the genuine philosophical element in every work, whether it be a work of art, of science, or of thought, is its capacity for elaboration, which Ludwig Feuerbach defined as *Entwicklungsfähigkeit*" (Giorgio Agamben, *The Signature of All Things*, trans. Luca D'Isanto with Kevin Attell [New York: Zone, 2009], 7-8. Photography is the technical apotheosis of developability.

6 Giorgio Agamben, *Stanzas: Word and Phantasm in Western Culture*, trans. Ronald L. Martinez (Minneapolis: University of Minnesota Press, 1993), 129.

exactly the no-thing between things that is all in all, the line that, being entirely nothing in itself, omnipresently touches each. That is what image *is*. Whence eros (love demanding the presence of the loved) as enlightening, levitating entanglement in something essentially linear–"Fortes tresses, soyez la houle qui m'enlève" [Strong tresses, be the swell that lifts me away][7]–and desire's imaging as art of lineation: kohl = focuser/refractor/deflector of ocular rays (NB: pupilization of the eye's outside, precise inversion of the veil's solar border); *Pondus meum amor meus*[8]–love as gravitational alignment (NB: black heart/dark star at bottom center); seductive collusions between writing, covering, and gaze, activator of eye as follower (line-linen-lingere) . . . Beauty is a total barzakhification of being, absolutization of the (in)visible line between light and dark: "The created realm is the *barzakh* between Light and darkness. In its essence it is qualified neither by darkness nor by Light, since it is the *barzakh* and the middle, having a property from each of its two sides. That is why He 'appointed' for man 'two eyes hennaed hands and our slender pointed nails, our double, our darkened image. The composition of the picture sets up this equivalence, this Iranian stand-off, conveying our gaze directly into the eye-line of the woman framed in the blackness of the veil. One eye, obscured behind the reflected flash of light, the other–the evil one, no doubt–looks directly at 'us', at me, behind thick eyeliner. "As we are about to take the final step, we are beside ourselves with desire, paralyzed, in the clutch of a force that demands our disintegration" (Bataille, *Erotism*: 141). Hands are held up against the translucent barrier and the dark figure behind it. What denotes the glass barrier, if it is glass, is the reflected light and, in the top left-hand corner, where the left index finger points, some painted writing. Whatever it is, writing signifies that there is Law somewhere, and here, as ever, it marks the point of separation, all points of separation, between light and dark, subject and viewer, beauty and its profanation, woman and woman. Because I must remember that the woman does not look at an 'us'. These hands at the foreground of the picture

---

[7] Charles Baudelaire, *The Flowers of Evil* (New York: Oxford, 1993), 'La Chevelure,' line 13.

[8] Augustine, *Confessions*, 13.9.

and guided him on the two highways' (Koran 90:8–10), for man exists between the two paths."[9] "Such a one, as soon as he beholds the beauty of this world, is reminded of true beauty, and his wings begin to grow."[10] **N**

address another woman–the photographer–as if in challenge and complicity, each woman looking the other in the eye. What do they see–each other's life, love and beauty, or death? In her place, my looking enacts her sacrifice. **S**

---

[9] Ibn Arabi, *al-Futûhât*, 1911 edition, 3:274.28, cited from William Chittick, 'Ibn Arabi,' *Stanford Encyclopedia of Philosophy*, <http://plato.stanford.edu/entries/ibn-arabi/>. "Know that the word *barzakh* is an expression for what *separates* two things without ever becoming either of them, such as the line separating a shadow from the sunlight, or as in His Saying--may He be exalted!: 'He has loosened the two Seas. They meet: / between them a *barzakh*, they do not go beyond' (55: 19-20)–meaning that neither of them becomes mixed with the other. But even if our senses are unable to perceive what separates those two things, the intellect judges that there is indeed a divider separating them--and that divider grasped by the intellect is precisely the *barzakh*. Because if something is perceived by the senses, it must be one of those two things, rather than the *barzakh*. So each of those two things, when they are adjacent to each other, have need of a *barzakh* which is not the same as each of them, but which has in itself the power of each of them" (Ibn Arabi, *al-Futûhât al-Makkîya* [The Meccan Illuminations], chapter 63, trans. James. W. Morris, forthcoming).

[10] *Phaedrus*, 249e, cited from *The Collected Dialogues of Plato*, eds. Edith Hamilton and Huntington Cairns (Princeton, NJ: Princeton University Press, 1961), 496. Plato elaborates: "For by reason of the stream of beauty entering in through his eyes there comes a warmth, whereby the soul's plumage is fostered, and with that the roots of the wings are melted, which for long had been so hardened and closed up that nothing could grow; then as the nourishment is poured in, the stump of the wing swells and hastens to grow from the root over the whole substance of the soul" (251b). *Cauda pavonis*, Melek Taus, elaboration of the colorful space between dark and light, nigredo and albedo, opening up of the original-final relation between wings and eyes: "And round the throne, on each side of the throne, are four living creatures, full of eyes in front and behind . . . And the four living creatures, each of them with six wings, are full of eyes all round and within" (Revelation 4:6-8).

003501

Desire and the drive: A Persian tale baked upon an arch made of brick. *Que vuoi?* I don't know anything about photography. I don't know anything about Kristen Alvanson except that she is American and has an Iranian partner. What does that have to do with anything? Are all these photographs taken in Iran? I don't know anything about Iran, couldn't identify a monument, square, rock. *We think you know a lot about desire.* This is the last, terrifying sentence on the email from N, inviting me to participate in this project. Who are *we*? And what do they suppose about my knowledge of desire? I've written on Lacan. But the page mock-up, determining the length of each gloss, consists entirely of repeated denunciations of psychoanalysis in favour of Deleuze and Guattari! Already my looking has been pre-directed by an imagined dichotomy I reject. This picture, the first one allotted to me, I cannot see now as anything but a staging of the question of desire, in a picture structured by a series of dualities, too many. But mainly: two planes and surfaces, ceramic tiles and whitewashed brick. I am struck by the awkwardness of the framing that truncates the images glazed on the tiles and makes the nature of the building difficult to read. (Already visual desire is provoked through a brutal act of photographic 'castration'!) Modern (Western) consumer desire finds its origin and definition in eighteenth-century Orientalism in a fantasy of despotism and Other jouissance: *The Arabian Knights* but also Montesquieu's *Persian Letters* (1721).[11] Scheherazade's 1001 glosses, wagering life on the desire of the Other, for "desire is interpretation itself" (Lacan, 4fcs, 176). Who is he, horseman of desire with his train of followers, is he laying siege or coming home to the golden citadel I imagine in the top corner, the point towards which all the lines tend? Visual desire is related to the scopic drive that is all the more deadly and machinic for being photographic, click after click, picture after picture, arching around a vacuole in brick-like, stolid satisfaction. But the desire that this drive supports, I wager (but we will see), is not to picture, objectify or possess Iran or Iranian objects, but to "operate on a sacrificial plane" and arouse Iranian desire itself, "for what makes the value of the icon is that the god it represents is also looking at it" (Lacan, 4fc: 113). **S**

[11] Which illustrates interestingly how the East and the West–the Orient and the Americas–could, in the 18th c., be related in a triangular structure that connected virtue with erotic and economic value.

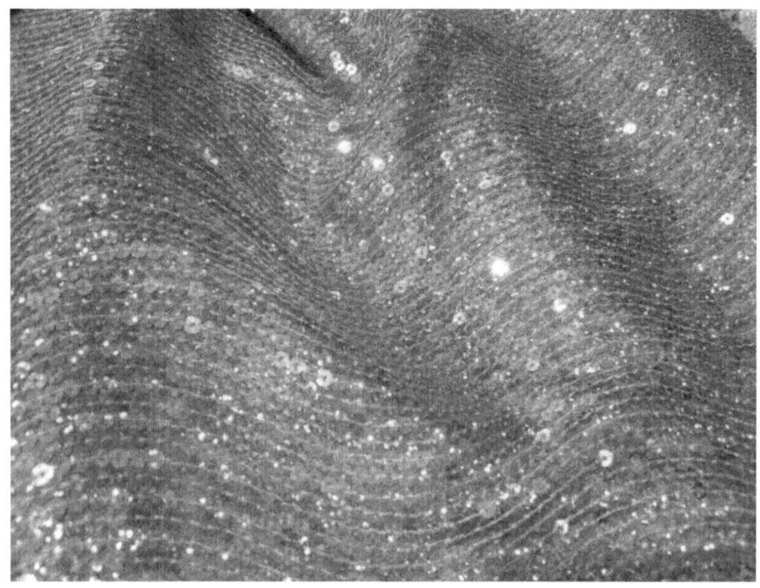

003510

CHAINS OF BEING.[12] But without hierarchical	SEQUINED SEA of space-time / the multiple / an apparition of

[12] "[S]ince Mind emanates from the Supreme God, and Soul from Mind, and Mind, indeed, forms and suffuses all below with life, and since this is the one **splendor** lighting up everything and visible in all, like a countenance reflected in many **mirrors** arranged in a row, and since all follow on in continuous succession, degenerating step by step [*degenerantia per ordinem*] in their downward course, the close observer will find that from the Supreme God even to the bottommost dregs of the universe [*a summo deo usque ad ultimam rerum faecem*] there is one tie [*conexio*], binding at every link and never broken. This is the golden chain [*catena aurea*] of Homer which, he tells us, God ordered to hang down from the sky to the earth" (Macrobius, *Commentary on the Dream of Scipio*, trans. William Harris Stahl [New York: Columbia University Press, 1952], 14.15). "The chain principle is an ontological wholism. It **threads** the fact of universe itself, expressing the inseparability of the *what* and the *that* [NOTE: The distinction does not happen to us arbitrarily or from time to time, but *fundamentally* and constantly. . . . For precisely in order to experience *what* and *how* beings in each case *are* in themselves as the beings that they *are*, we must–although not conceptually–already understand something like the what-being [*Was-sein*] and the that-being [*Dass-sein*] of beings. . . . We never ever experience

(de)generation, and like the weird placeless place we see ourselves in (universe), without center or edge. Those are projections of perspective, ocular ego, the cameral eye that, judging all in the space of its body-forms. Immersed, neither inside nor out, how can I tell that this doesn't go on forever? Undulating, an iridescent mirage that discloses nothing but desert without end or horizon reaching from the earth to the farthest

anything about being subsequently or after the event from beings; rather beings–wherever and however we approach them–*already* stand *in the light of being*. In the metaphysical sense, therefore, the distinction stands at the commencement of Dasein itself. . . . Man, therefore, always has the possibility of asking: What is that? And Is it at all or is it not?" (Martin Heidegger, *The Fundamental Concepts of Metaphysics: World, Finitude, Solitude*, trans. William McNeill and Nicholas Walker [Bloomington: Indiana University Press, 1995], 357)]. The cosmic *catena* is the necessary point of identity, **piercing** every entity, between essence and existence, the invisible thing making it so that everything is next to something else and part of everything itself. It is thus in a full and total sense the *chain of being*, the fact of being's being a chain or binding: at once the universal necessity of the actuality of the everything (the fact that there is such a thing as everything) and the individual necessity of the actuality of individuation (the fact that each thing is inexorably shackled to itself) [NOTE: "Why am I me? A stupid question. . . . I am too stupid to answer this question. And to ask it, just stupid enough. What is the mechanism of such stupid questioning? I imagine a small organ, neither inside nor outside myself, like a polymelic phantom limb, a subtle psychic appendage implanted at birth behind my crown, during the moment of my coming to be, whenever that was. This organ (or appendix, or tumor), whose painful inflammation is despair–'despair is the paroxysm of individuation' (Cioran)–is like a strange supplementary bodily member, intimate and inessential, which I can feel yet not move, barely move yet without feeling. Stupid organ, organ of stupidity. It moves, is moved, like an inalienable shackle, only to reinforce its immobility. Am I to sever this organ, hemorrhage of haecceity, escape it? '[E]scape is the need to get out of oneself, that is, *to break that most radical and unalterably binding of chains, the fact that the I [moi] is oneself [soi-même]*' (Levinas). Just *who*, then, would escape?" (Nicola Masciandaro, "Individuation: This Stupidity," *Postmedieval* 1 [2010], forthcoming). "The act whereby being–existence–is bestowed upon us is an *unbearable* surpassing of being" (Bataille)]. The chain encompasses from within the impossible unity of perspective on being that cosmos presupposes: the definite vision of the unbounded whole from the position of one-sided asymmetry occupied by the individual" (Nicola Masciandaro, "Anti-Cosmosis: Black Mahapralaya," in *Hideous Gnosis: Black Metal Theory Symposium 1*, ed. Nicola Masciandaro [New York: 2010], 71-3, my emphasis in bold).

chamber, is bound to frame things, above all the frameless, to capitalize what it cannot see crossing: "The human being arrives at the threshold: there he must throw himself headlong [*vivant*] into that which has no foundation and has no head."[13] Hence: the cosmological principle (homogeneity & isotrophy). Yet: "the world does not consist of infinitely many essentially identical things–atoms moving in space–but is in reality a collection of infinitely many things, each constructed according to a common principle yet all different from one another. Space and time emerge from the way in which these ultimate entities *mirror* each other."[14] And: "Picture yourself as drops, and your body as bubbles inside the ocean. Now, each of you drops sees neither your own drop-state nor the drop-state of others. You see your own bubbles and bubbles of others, and this large bubble of heavens, extending to remotest space, countless particles multiplied as often as there are leaves in the forest, feathers upon birds, scales on fish, drops of water in the mighty ocean, atoms in the vast expanse of the air . . . How much do I love thee? Let me count the ways . . . Love is of course the immeasurable and the unaccountable. It's not the sequins that she wears, it's not her baby-fine blond hair, it's more the desert in her stare (Iggy Pop). The truth of desire discloses itself as nothing but semblance. But what is this auto-disclosure? Desire of course transcends the object, directed by the semblance of being immanent to it. Desire is always directed towards another desire which, without mediation or regulation, replicates itself endlessly in sequences so that desire is desire of desire of desire of desire of desire of desire . . . Not signifiers but sequins: no longer *zecchino*, medium of exchange, but pure

[13] Georges Bataille, "The Obelisk," in *Visions of Excess: Selected Writings, 1927-1939*, trans. Allan Stoekl (Minneapolis: University of Minnesota Press, 1985), 222. "L' être humain arrive au seuil: là il est nécessaire de se précipiter vivant dans ci qui n'a plus d'assise ni de tête" (*Oeuvres Completes*, 12 vols. [Paris: Gallimard, 1970-88], 1: 13).

[14] Julian Barbour, *The End of Time: The Next Revolution in our Understanding of the Universe* (London: Weidenfeld and Nicolson, 1999), 240, cited from "The View from Nowhen: Interview with Julian Barbour," *Collapse V* (2009): 108, my emphasis.

the world."[15] Until you finally find yourself: "that last amorphous blight of nethermost confusion which blasphemes and bubbles at the center of all infinity."[16] Following the sequins, a bubble-catena is in order.[17] Led metonymy, pure sequentiality without order of priority or narrative, flickering in the full nothingness of evacuated exchange-value, the empty plenitude of digitality. Who could make a metaphor of it?

---

[15] Meher Baba, cited from Bhau Kalchuri, *Meher Prabhu*, 14 vols. (Myrtle Beach, SC: Manifestation, 1980), 8.2885, commenting in 1943 on a version of the following chart.

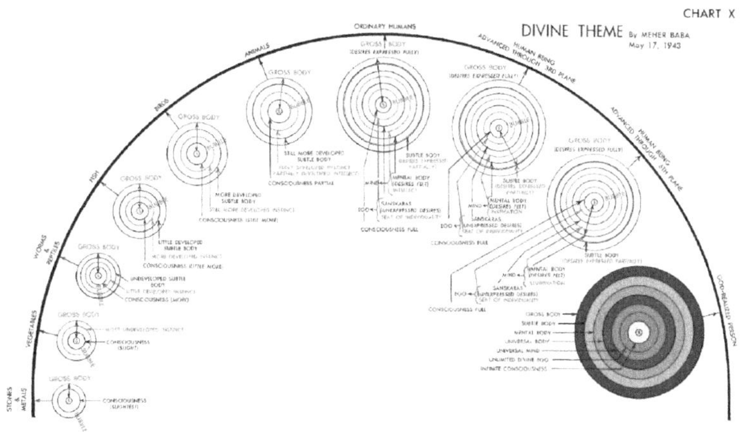

[16] H. P. Lovecraft, *The Dream Quest of Unknown Kadath*, in *The Dreams in the Witchhouse and Other Weird Stories* (New York: Penguin, 2004), 156.

[17] "A somewhat surprising application of fermentation to cosmology . . ." (Walter Pagel, *Joan Baptista Van Helmont: Reformer of Science and Medicine* [Cambridge: Cambridge University Press, 1985], 85, describing Gottfried Wilhelm Leibniz's *Hypothesis physica nova* (1671), wherein "divine ether is made to penetrate the major part of matter, which becomes the earth, and to be enclosed in *bullae* [bubbles]"). "Unicorns do not exist, but a soap bubble would burst were it punctured by a unicorn horn" (John Heil, *From An Ontological Point of View* [Oxford: Oxford University Press, 2003], 221). "And even to me, one who likes life, it seems butterflies and soap bubbles and whatever is of their kind among human beings know most about happiness" (Friedrich Nietzsche, *Thus Spoke Zarathustra*, trans. Adrian Del Caro [Cambridge: Cambridge University Press, 2006], 28). "There will be no *social* solution to the present situation. First, because the vague aggregate of social milieus, institutions, and individualized bubbles that is called, with a touch of

---

antiphrasis, "society," has no consistency" (The Invisible Committee, *The Coming Insurrection*, *<http://tarnac9.wordpress.com/texts/the-coming-insurrection/>*). "The innocent cruelty; the opaque monstrosity of eyes scarcely distinguishable from the little bubbles that form on the surface of mud; the horror as integral to life as light is to a tree" (Georges Bataille, *Encyclopedia Acephalica: Comprising the Critical Dictionary and Related Texts*, trans. Iain White [London: Atlas, 1996], s.v. "Metamorphosis"). ". . . these and many other instances which could be given prove that indeed the personal consciousness is but a bubble floating on the tide of Being, and liable, at any moment of strong emotion, to be swept into nothingness" (Oliver H. P. Smith, "Evolution and Consciousness," *The Monist* 9 [1899]: 231). "The devout soul is a fountain which glides and flows, and which ever springs up anew, because it is renewed in God. It never ceases to bubble forth, and break out in love for Him, to swell for its own needs, and to expand itself in affection for its neighbor" (Richard of Saint Victor, cited from Richard Frederick Littledale, *A Commentary on the Song of Songs, from Ancient and Medieval Sources* [London: Joseph Masters, 1869], 192). "The bubble was formed from water, in water it disappears" ('Abd al-Quddus, Cited from Scott Alan Kugle, *Sufis & Saints's Bodies: Mysticism, Corporeality, & Sacred Power in Islam* [Chapel Hill, NC: University of North Carolina Press, 2007], 246). "But elsewhere, deeper in the granite, are there certain chambers that have no entrances? Chambers never unsealed since the arrival of the gods. Local report declares that these exceed in number those that can be visited, as the dead exceed the living–four hundred of them, four thousand or million. Nothing is inside them, they were sealed up before the creation of pestilence or treasure; if mankind grew curious and excavated, nothing, nothing would be added to the sum of good or evil. One of them is rumoured within the boulder that swings on the summit of the highest of the hills; a bubble-shaped cave that has neither ceiling nor floor, and mirrors its own darkness in every direction infinitely" (E. M. Forster, *A Passage to India* [Orlando: Harcourt, 1984], 136). "Animals and plants come into being in earth and in liquid because there is water in earth, and air in water, and in all air is vital heat so that in a sense all things are full of soul. Therefore living things form quickly whenever this air and vital heat are enclosed in anything. When they are so enclosed, the corporeal liquids being heated, there arises as it were a frothy bubble" (Aristotle, *On the Generation of Animals*, trans. Arthur Platt, <http://ebooks.adelaide.edu.au/a/aristotle/generation/>). "As in the multiple worlds view, the spacetime sheet separates into two opposing curvatures, resulting in a 'bubble' or 'blister' in underlying reality" (Stewart R. Hameroff and Jonathan Powell, "The Conscious Connection: A Psycho-Physical Bridge Between Brain and Pan-Experiential Quantum Geometry," in *Mind That Abides: Panpsychism in the New Millenium*, ed. David Skrbina [Amsterdam: John Benjamins, 2009], 117). "Imagine the infinitely unconscious God state A, before the Creation came into being, as motionless infinite ocean. A puff of by its thread, I return nowhere. Unless the line belongs to Ariadne, bride of Dionysius, unless I am moved: "A l'alta fantasia qui mancò possa; / ma già volgeva il mio disio e 'l velle, / sì come rota ch'igualmente è mossa, / l'amor che move il sole e l'altre stele."[18] Then something else happens: the shockingly silent current of a being so deeply outside that touching it short-

Who would turn this multiple into the likeness of One? She puts on a universe comprised entirely of sequins strings, patterns emerge–life seems to glisten in *semblants* of being–in folds and clusters, in degrees of intensity, in the fabric of space/time, to arouse the desire of God, who names her the Universe, the One. But she is *la belle noiseuse*, querulous beauty

wind then stirred the tranquil uniformity of this ocean, and immense waves, countless drops of water, and innumerable bubbles appeared from out of the uniformity of the limitless, infinite ocean. The puff of wind that set the ocean into commotion may be compared to the impulse of the infinite, original urge-to-know originating with the infinite, orginal whim of God, surging in God to know Himself through His infinite God State II. The stir on the surface of the ocean, caused by the infinite urge, surcharged every drop of that infinite ocean with the infinite urge-to-know itself. Thus *Paramatma* [Over-Soul] in His infinitely unconscious state A, being urged to know Himself, simultaneously bestirs the tranquil poise of every *atma* [soul] in *Paramatma* with an urge to know itself. This could only be understood when *Paramatma* is compared to an infinite ocean and the *atmas* to the drops of that infinite ocean. But it must also be well noted that every drop of the ocean, when in the ocean, is ocean itself, until the drops inherit individuality through bubble formations over the surface of the ocean. Every bubble thus formed would then bestow a separate and a particular individuality upon every drop. And this created separateness would exist with the uniform indivisibility of the drops of the infinite ocean as long as these bubbles creating separateness exist. As soon as the bubbles burst, the drops, which are and were already in the ocean itself, come to realize that they are and were one with the infinite ocean; and they gain this consciousness of the **eternal infinity in the infinite ocean** only after they first experience separateness and then dispel the bubbles of ignorance that were instrumental in bestowing upon them the experience of their apparent separateness from their inherent indivisibility" (Meher Baba, *God Speaks: The Theme of Creation and Its Purpose*, 2nd ed. [New York: Dodd, Mead & Co., 1973], 182-3, original emphasis).

[18] Dante Alighieri, *The Divine Comedy*, ed. Charles Singleton (Princeton, NJ: Princeton University Press, 1977), *Paradiso* 33.142-5. [Here power failed the lofty phantasy; but already my desire and my will were revolved, like a wheel that is evenly moved, by the love which moves the sun and the other stars].

circuits interiority by keeping it all the more intact, so that everything intensifies contact by staying right where it is, accelerating individuation's thrilling spin: "Individuation as such, as it operates beneath all forms, in inseparable from a pure ground that it brings to the surface and trails with it. It is difficult to describe this ground, or the terror and attraction it excites."[19] Here one disk flashes above all the others, becoming solar.[20] And this is due only to the undulation of the (w)hole, the movement of everything within its own emptiness. Physicist says, "We must understand how the universe can 'swim in nothing'."[21] Waves. Wave is how ocean swims, so that somewhere, somehow, somewhen, "Wave, sea and bubble, all three are one."[22] **N**

(Serres), flashing eyes and glinting hatred: noisily not (not) one she ex-sists in the domain of the infinite with which she is continuous. Glistening jouissance, pure surface - not of the repetitive circuit of the drive (the brickwork, the crumbling walls, the undead historical process that goes nowhere) but in the *en-corps* (Lacan) which insists in the body beyond its sexual being (Seminar XX 26/23). "It is in the traces of jouissance inscribed in this *en-corps* that we can, perhaps, discern something of the *poesis*–the something coming from nothing–that Lacan links to the contingency of being and, ultimately, to the path of love" (Suzanne Bernard). **S**

---

[19] Gilles Deleuze, *Difference and Repetition*, trans. Paul Patton. (New York: Columbia, 1994), 152.

[20] I.e. instantaneous participation "in the Project of Tellurian Omega, where the Earth reaches utter immanence with its burning core - or the metal core of the tellurian real - and the Sun" (Reza Negarestani, *Cyclonopedia: Complicity with Anonymous Materials* [Melbourne: re.press, 2008], 45).

[21] "The View from Nowhen: Interview with Julian Barbour," *Collapse V* (2009): 117. "Seeing something simply in its being-thus–irreparable, but not for that reason necessary; thus, but not for that reason contingent–is love" (Giorgio Agamben, *The Coming Community*, trans. Michael Hardt [Minneapolis: University of Minnesota Press, 1993], 105).

[22] Shah Nimatullah Wali, cited from Leonard Lewisohn, *The Heritage of Sufism, Volume II: The Legacy of Mediaeval Persian Sufism (1150-1500)* (Oxford: Oneworld Publications, 1999), xviii. Cf. "The hyperlocality of the Cosmos is the feature of the Cosmos causing instantaneous geometrical change either on

003543

THOUGHT IS WAR. In one noetic stroke I 'mak siccar' my tanist ascension-succession to the throne of blood,[23] suffer decollation by

the scale of the Cosmos itself or between volumes of space not locally connected by matter but connected only by the vacuum bubbles of the cosmic foam. The whole of physical space across the entire Cosmos has a vibrating topology (vibrations too small to be physically detected) caused by the undulation of all of the Cosmos's composite vacuum bubbles connected in one seamless continuum. This is the hyperlocality of the Cosmos" (Kip K. Sewell, *The Cosmic Sphere* [New York: Nova Science, 1999], 120).

[23] "The ancient succession of Scotland had been by tanistry, that is, the monarchy was elective within a small group of kinsmen, the descendants of Macalpine. In consequence, the king was almost as a matter of course assassinated by his successor, who chose the moment most favourable to himself to 'make siccar' an inheritance that could never be regarded as assured . . . by tanist law Macbeth had as good a claim as Duncan, and his wife a rather better one" (M.C. Bradbrook, "The Sources of *Macbeth*," in *Shakespeare Survey 4: Interpretation*, ed. Allardyce Nicoll [Cambridge: Cambridge University Press, 1951], 38). Here is a telling of Robert Bruce's killing of John Comyn in the Franciscan church at Dumfries that allegorizes perfectly unintentionally the binary verbo-violent dynamism of murder (Cf. "Roussillon waited until Cabestanh was at close range, then he rushed out at

him with murder and destruction in his heart, brandishing a lance above his head and shouting: 'Traitor, you are dead!' And before the words were out of his mouth he had driven the lance through Cabestanh's breast. Cabestanh was powerless to defend himself, or even to utter a word, on being run through by the lance he fell to ground" [Boccaccio, *Decameron*, trans. G.H. McWilliam (New York: Penguin, 1972), 4.9]) as *thought's endless war of succession around the boundary of doubt and certainty*: "They embraced and kissed each other, after the manner of the times, with a glow of friendliness, and then walked up the church together towards the high altar, engaged, as it seemed, in earnest conversation. As they advanced their words grew high and keen. Bruce accused Comyn of having betrayed him to Edward. 'You lie!" said the impudent traitor. Bruce, without a word more, drew his dagger and struck him down on the very steps of the altar. It was the outburst of a moment. Bruce instantly felt shocked at the rash deed. He rushed to his friends, who waited him outside church. 'I doubt,' he said, 'that I have slain the Comyn!' 'You doubt;' cried Sir Roger Kirkpatrick; 'I mak siccar;' and running into the church, he dispatched the wretched man with repeated wounds. 'When you kill a man, do it well,' says the Koran; which also seems to have been the opinion of Sir Roger" (James Mackenzie, *The History of Scotland* [London: Nelson and Sons, 1867], 131-2). Note the uncanny opining of the word of God as internal engine and hermeneutic limit of the event. Corollary: thinking is the material where divine logos enters as weapon: "For the word of God is living and active, sharper than any two-edged sword, piercing to the division of soul and spirit, of joints and marrow, and discerning [κριτικός] the thoughts and intentions of the heart" (Hebrews 4:12). Whence criticism as cutting word (dis-cernere), self-naming of an awakened one the ultimate weapon: "MUAD'DIB: *[thinks]* My own name is a killing word. Will it be a healing word as well?" (*Dune*, dir. David Lynch [1984]). Commentary as weirding module. "See now that I, even I, am he, and there is no god beside me; I kill and I make alive; I wound and I heal; and there is none that can deliver out of my hand. . . . I will make my arrows drunk with blood, and my sword shall devour flesh–with the blood of the slain and the captives, from the long-haired heads of the enemy" (Deuteronomy 32:39-42). Playing God, the critic rains arrows on the globe: "Ad mundum mitto mea iacula, dumque sagitto; / At vbi iustus erit, nulla sagitta ferit. / Sed male viuentes hos vulnero transgredientes; / Conscius ergo sibi se speculetur ibi" [I send my darts at the world and simultaneously shoot arrows; / But mind you, wherever there is a just man, no one will receive arrows. / I badly wound those living in transgression, however; / Therefore, let the thoughtful man look out for himself] (John Gower, *Minor Latin Works*, ed. and trans. R.F. Yeager [Kalamazoo, Michigan: Medieval Institute Publications, 2005])–no collateral damage. These lines from the frontispiece to the *Vox Clamantis*:

Whence bombs as percussive prophecy: smart missiles raining wrath and reform on the earth (shock & awe), self-detonating auto-decapitating "voice[s] of one crying in the desert" (Mark 1:3) – all profanely belated heralds of presumed last prophets, martyrs (death-witnesses) to their own living deaths. But this photograph shuts my eyes to looking from either idealized end, to seeing the explosion arrive from heaven or earth. Here I no longer watch through the lens of the either/or, the filter of enemy/friend. Locating me on the endless continuum of the middle, in the living space of subtitular existence between two spear points that never touch ("Then the king gat his spear in both his hands, and ran toward Sir Mordred, crying: Traitor, now is thy death-day come. And when Sir Mordred heard Sir Arthur, he ran until him with his sword drawn in his hand. And there King Arthur smote Sir Mordred under the shield, with a foin of his spear, throughout the body, more than a fathom. And when Sir Mordred felt that he had his death wound he thrust himself with the might that he had up to the bur of King Arthur's spear. And right so he smote his father Arthur, with his sword holden in both his hands, on the side of the head, that the sword pierced the helmet and the brain-pan, and therewithal Sir Mordred fell stark dead to the earth; and the noble Arthur fell in a swoon to the earth, and there he swooned ofttimes" Malory *Le Morte D'Arthur*), it shows the real case (*casus*, befalling event): here the sword of Damocles,[24] martyrically live to tell the tale,[25] and wander the burnt plains of being . . . a cephalophore: "Di sé facea a sé

everyone is 'taken out.' "When you're wounded and left on Afghanistan's plains, / And the women come out to cut up what remains, / Jest roll to your rifle and blow out your brains / An' go to your Gawd like a soldier" (Rudyard Kipling, "The Young British Soldier," *War Stories and Poems*, [Oxford: Oxford University Press, 1990], 56).

[24] "This tyrant [Dionysius II of Syracuse], however, showed himself how happy he really was; for once, when Damocles, one of his flatterers, was dilating in conversation on his forces, his wealth, the greatness of his power, the plenty he enjoyed, the grandeur of his royal palaces, and maintaining that no one was ever happier,' Have you an inclination,' said he, 'Damocles, as this kind of life pleases you, to have a taste of it yourself, and to make a trial of the good fortune that attends me?' And when he said that he should like it extremely, Dionysius ordered him to be laid on a bed of gold with the most beautiful covering, embroidered and wrought with the most exquisite work, and he dressed out a great many sideboards with silver and embossed gold. He then ordered some youths, distinguished for their handsome persons, to wait at his table, and to observe his nod, in order to serve him with what he wanted. There were ointments and garlands; perfumes were burned; tables provided with the most exquisite meats. Damocles thought himself very happy. In the midst of this apparatus, Dionysius ordered a bright sword to be let down from the ceiling, suspended by a single horse-hair, so as to hang over the head of that happy man. After which he neither cast his eye on those handsome waiters, nor on the well-wrought plate; nor touched any of the provisions: presently the garlands fell to pieces. At last he entreated the tyrant to give him leave to go, for that now he had no desire to be happy" (Cicero, *Tusculan Disputations*, trans. C.D. Young [New York: Harper, 1899], ch.21).

[25] "Instantly the body of Saint Dionysius stood up, took his head in his arms . . ." (Jacobus de Voragine, *The Golden Legend: Readings on the Saints*, trans. William Granger Ryan, 2 vols [Princeton: Princeton University Press, 1993], 2.240). "Tunc erigens se sancti viri corpus exanime, apprehendit propriis manibus sanctum caput abscissum" [Raising itself, the lifeless body of the holy man then grasped with his own hands the sacred severed head] (Odone, *De sanctis martyribus Luciano episcopo, Maximiano presbytero, Iuliano diacono*, 5.21, *Acta Sanctorum Database* [ProQuest]). "*Ubi es?* ecce, mirabile auditu, caput martyris patria lingua respondebat dicens, *Heer, Heer, Heer*; quod est interpretatum, *Hic, Hic, Hic*" [*Where are you?* Behold, marvelous to hear, the head of the martyr responded in his native language, *Heer, Heer, Heer*, which is to say, *Here, Here, Here*] (Abbo of Fleury, *Passio Sancti Eadmundi*, cited from *Corolla Sancti Eadmundi*, ed. Lord Francis Harvey [London: John Murray, 1907], 566). On John the Baptist: "The original martyr (witness) is neither a martyr nor not a martyr. He dies neither for the sake of what he testifies to nor not for the sake of what he testifies to. The original martyrdom is instead

stesso lucerna, / ed eran due in uno e uno in due; / com' esser può, qui sa che sì governa . . . levò 'l braccio alto con tutta la testa / per appressarne le parole sue, che fuoro: '. . . Così s'osserva in me lo contrapasso'" (*Inferno* 28.124-42).[26] Bertran's bellophilic body–"Que nuills om non es ren prezatz / Tro q'a maintz colps pres e donatz"[27]–displays the logic of war's dyadic vortexical intensity (2-becoming-1-becoming-2 *in perpetuo*: "He [Indra, war] can no more be reduced to one or the other than he can constitute a third of their kind")[28] as

the supreme death of the supreme witness in relation to which other martyrs stay original, i.e. remain in proximity to their unrepeatable origin. It is the death of one who cannot survive his witnessing and the witnessing of one who cannot not die. John's identity is a severed identity which becomes the seed ensuring that each following death is a witnessing and that each following witness must die, the a-martyric ovum holding the Christian meaning of *martyr*. What enables this generation is John's uncanny intimacy–'There was a man sent from God whose name was John' (John 1:6)–with what he absolutely cannot be, with what he *must* say he is not: 'I am not the Christ' (John 1:20). In a strange and unspeakable way, the martyric meaning of John's beheading poetically approaches its precise impossibility. It becomes the performance of exactly what it can never be, the necessarily decapitative murder of the theological traitor, the killing of the one who says *I am God* [cf. Mansur al-Hallaj]" (Nicola Masciandaro, "*Non potest hoc corpus decollari*: Beheading and the Impossible," in *Heads Will Roll: Decapitation in Medieval Literature and Culture*, eds. Larissa Tracy and Jeff Massey [University Press of Florida, forthcoming]).

[26] "Of itself it was making a lamp of itself, and they were two in one and one in two – how this can be, He knows who so ordains. . . . he raised high his arm with the head, in order to bring near to us his words, which were, '. . . Thus is the retribution observed in me.'"

[27] "For no man is worth a damn till he has taken and given many a blow" (Bertran de Born, "Bem platz lo gais temps de pascor," trans. Ezra Pound, cited from *Lark in the Morning: The Verses of the Troubadours*, ed. Robert Kehew [Chicago: University of Chicago Press, 2005], 142-3]).

[28] Deleuze & Guattari, *A Thousand Plateaus*, trans. Brian Massumi (Minneapolis: University of Minnesota Press, 1987), 352). D&G's "can no more" corresponds to Dante's "e" [and], which joins by holding separate "uno in due" and "due in uno." I.e. Bertran is precisely not *both* 1-in-2 and 2-in-1, but the *and* of their non-intersecting identity, the touch of the split or heresy-choice that makes them. Cf. "Severing also is still a joining and a relating" ("[A]uch das Trennen ist noch ein Verbinden und Beziehen" (Martin Heidegger, "Logik: Heraklits Lehre vom Logos," in *Heraklit*, 'Gesamtausgabe,' Bd. 55 [Frankfurt am Main: Vittorio Klostermann, 1970], 337).

thought's essential gesture: holding forth a speaking head. Raising the arm to press words towards another (*ad-pressare*) is a haptic nexus of striking and speaking that indicates war to be the writing of thought's weight on all bodies, a bloody texting of the general violence of dissatisfied embodiment: "war does not embody any special suffering. People really suffer all the time. They suffer because they are not satisfied–they want more and more. War is more an outcome of the universal suffering of dissatisfaction than an embodiment of representative suffering."[29] War does not typify suffering, but is the very writing of suffering that thought constitutes as its/our splitting-choosing (*haereses*) into desire/dream/reality.[30] "Writing is the dissimulation of the natural, primary, and immediate presence of sense to the soul within the logos. Its violence befalls the soul as unconsciousness."[31] Consciousness is the unconscious of war.[32] Your thoughts are its subtitles. And if thy head offend thee, cut it off, and cast it from thee: for it is profitable for thee that one of thy members should perish, and not that thy whole body should be cast into hell (Cf. Matthew 5:30). The fog of war rises from black-biled earth, humus/humour, dark with organic matter for thought. War-genius is melancholic, a thought-sufferer, knower of its passions.[33] And plunges

[29] Meher Baba, *Discourses*, 3.10.

[30] Cf. the schismatic community of Dante's ninth *bolgia* to which Bertran de Born belongs, headed by arch-self-splitter Mohammed, who identifies himself as a visual third-person: "Mentre che tutto in lui veder m'attacoo, / guardommi e con le man s'aperse il petto, dicendo: 'Or vedi com' io mi dilacco! / vedi come storpiato è Mäometto!" (*Inferno* 238.28-31) [While I was all aborbed in gazing on him, he looked at me and with his hands pulled open his breast, saying, "Now see how I rend myself, see how mangled is Mohammed!"]

[31] Jacques Derrida, *Of Grammatology*, trans. Gayatri Chakravorty Spivak (Baltimore: Johns Hopkins University Press, 1976), 37.

[32] "Get on the ground! Get on the fucking ground! Now! [Thinking] This great evil. Where's it come from? How'd it steal into the world? What seed, what root did it grow from? Who's doing this? Who's killing us?" (*The Thin Red Line*, dir. Terrence Malick [1998]).

[33] "Lastly, we come to men who are difficult to move but have strong feelings–men who are to the previous type [choleric] like heat to a shower of sparks. These are the men who are best able to summon the titanic strength it takes to clear away the enormous burdens that obstruct activity in war. Their emotions move as great masses do––slowly but irresistibly" (Carl von Clausewitz, *On War*, trans. Michael Howard and Peter Paret [Oxford: Oxford University Press, 2007], 53). Kleemeier comments: "A melancholic in the

us back in: "the emerging battlespace–the *intermezzo* where/in we make contact with the SIMAD–is a locale in which an ungrounding of the Earth is in process and, as such, is a vertiginous soft spot on the surface of the Earth."[34]

Clausewitzian sense is . . . someone who will act in exactly the right way, because his passions form a strong and solid foundation for action. So melancholy is not an illness at all, but a source of successful action. There is a certain ring of paradox here. On the one hand, you cannot eliminate the element of suffering from the notion of passion (*Leidenschaft*). Having a passion, as distinct from having a spontaneous emotion or affection, means being driven by a constant and powerful mental need, and to be in permanent need of something certainly indicates suffering. On the other hand, passions can become the very basis of great actions. This is so, because passions can combine with reason in a way spontaneous feelings cannot. . . . The link between passion and reason is will power" (Ulrike Kleemeir, "Moral Forces in War," in *Clausewitz in the Twenty-First Century*, eds. Hew Strachan and Andreas Herber-Rothe [Oxford: Oxford University Press, 2007], 112-3). Cf. "In most persons the mind accepts ends from the promptings of wants, but this means denial of the life of the spirit. Only when the mind accepts its ends and values from the deepest promptings of the heart does it contribute to the life of the spirit. Thus mind has to work in co-operation with the heart; factual knowledge has to be subordinated to intuitive perceptions; and heart has to be allowed full freedom in determining the ends of life without any interference from the mind" (Meher Baba, *Discourses*, 1.140).

[34] Manabrata Guha, "Introduction to SIMADology: *Polemos* in the 21st Century," *Collapse VI: Geo/Philosophy* (2010): 327.

003505

A trunk and a package of junk, tied with string. Let's go. They do not move. 'S' is the letter that denotes me in this glossing game. And here is 'my' letter stencilled on a cardboard box flattened to provide some loose casing for–what–wrought iron gates, a fence? This picture, which falls to me by the law of numerical series and sequencing that allots my place, has 'my' letter on it prominently placed and underlined. But of course this picture has absolutely nothing to do with me. I have never seen this alley, street or those objects. Then again, what does the letter 'S' have to do with me? Arbitrarily, according to the rules of the game, I am put into the picture as the letter 'S', a letter as alien to me as this picture. Has someone arrived or are they about to travel? Has someone died?[35] 'S' is visible but at the expense of 'me' who am absent, like the owner of these objects. "The signifier, whose first purpose is to bar the subject, has brought into him the meaning of death. (The letter kills, but we learn this from the letter itself)" (Lacan, Ecr. 848). The letter marks the point of division wherein one locates one's place as an effect of the chain, SAEND, arranged in couples at four corners, "in a form homologous to a pyramid", a tomb.[36] It is this form of fatal couplings that determines the destiny, if not the destination, of 'my' desire in the

---

[35] When I first saw this image I was reminded of Freud's tattered hat and coat that hangs above a weather-beaten monogrammed suitcase in the Freud Museum in Vienna. These signs of imminent departure are virtually all that is left of Freud in the house from which he fled from the Nazis. Almost everything in that house is now in Hampstead. But these objects did not leave, they were abandoned.

[36] This refers to the five-pointed geometrical form that structures the *dESIRE Gloss*: "Imagine a pentagram with vertices SAEND, in order of the continuous tracing of their five-pointed star. Each vertex represents a 'who' or person. The form is homologous to a pyramid (square + point suspended above it). Imagine ten continuous tracings of all the lines joining these vertices: S-A-E-N-D-S-E-D-A-N-S x 10 (each dash corresponds to a line between vertices; the first five trace the star, the second five trace the pentagonal perimeter). This is a geometrical representation of a unit (100) of intangible dESIRES in a form that communicates each desire as a line or force between two points. This form simultaneously articulates how: 1) desire always comes bundled with other desires; 2) how desire subsists as a circulation within such bundles; 3) how desire is essentially personal, involved with desire to be desired, a mode of answering *who am i?* Furthermore, as an iteration (10, 10, 10, . . . = 100), the form communicates how desire exists as a repetition of itself. Whence desire as the ground of habit, as opposed to whim or *incognitum hactenus*, which is absolutely spontaneous and utopically free. By commentarially submitting ourselves to such an arbitrary (?) regimen or absolute regularization of desire, we seriously/ridiculously desire to collectively realize, like monks in conjoined cells, desire's inherent freedom. This freedom is anticipated in the structure of the photograph as an undetermined determination of a relation between subject and object, a purely commentarial or deictic act (look!). Dialogic (or double-sided or self-mirroring or Narcissistic or *Romandelaroseian* or speculative, i.e. so beautiful that it does not at all resemble itself, what Guillaume de Lorris gives as birdsong 'Qu'il ne sembloit pas chans d'oisiaus') commentary, commentary on one object by two voices/selves, thus has the potential to realize all at once the nature of the image, the origination of anything/everything as our ownmost ecstasy, and the practice of photography as the technic-erotic perpetuation of love-at-first-sight."

context of this game. Appropriately the image seems to comprise, again, of a series of dualities: a dark alley, an opening, where all the lines tend, into the light. Propped up against the wall, the objects look set to travel, but just sit there. This could simply be a pile of rubbish. I see a couple, although there are many more than two objects: the sealed trunk, smug, inscrutable, sphinx-like; the other(s) ragged, dishevelled, letting it all (nearly) hang out. A game of even and odd, odd couples: Oscar and Felix, Jacques and Jacques, Félix and Gilles, Didi and Gogo. (Didigogo? No, he did not move. Yet desire is movement even in stasis; it is anticipation, imaginary flight, fantasy).[37] I see a trunk and a wrought iron-cardboard-string machine bearing a letter that has arrived by chance, as always, at its destination. **S**

[37] 'By The Time I Get to Phoenix' is a song of imaginary flight. It is another repetition in a series of failed departures–"I've left that girl so many times before." His anticipation is always displaced by nostalgia, the (love) sickness for home. "By the time I get to Phoenix, she'll be . . ." but he never gets to Phoenix.

003506

“In the mirror I discover my absence from the place where I am” (Foucault). A photographer, is this *the* photographer, Kristen Alvanson? At first sight, naively, it looks like a photograph of a woman, the street behind her, taking a photo of some desirable object in a shop window. But it could be a reflection, yes, the glass is angled relative to the picture plane; the photographer is the ‘desirable object’ looking at herself in the ‘shop window’. Even if it is not a reflection, this is the ruse of the double, setting up the desire to photograph the photographer looking at herself looking at herself. And here I am like her–like anyone–in the place where she discovers her absence, looking at herself looking at herself. The place of the shopper and the commodity is the same. Her left eye, not the camera lens, seems to look into that space from which she is now absent and from which I am looking, being drawn into this play of glances, this exchange of narcissisms. It is a look of intimacy, but it is not intimate. A smile plays on the photographer’s lips as she glances at herself and through herself into the virtual point, the empty space not of symbolic mediation but economic exchange, from which I look back at her. I notice the fractures in the glass hinting at the disunity of the body that is normally veiled by the specular image but is here disclosed. I fragment in turn. This commentary is too facile, don't you think? I see a hurried yet studied impersonation of feminine desire. On impulse, she pulls back the thick curtain, as heavy as death, unwinds her veil, takes a quick snap of something that catches her eye (herself). Transgressive feminine jouissance is on display even as it takes place out of the sight of the King and his police (Purloined Letter). It is not an image of female narcissism, but an advertising of feminine desire and jouissance that appeals to the narcissism of the viewer, his idiotic cleverness. This is desire pimping itself in the form of its own semblance all the better to remain hidden. Abject, I don't know how long I can go on playing the role of the (Lacanian) punter. It is time to unwind that veil, but what is behind it? Nothing but another semblance of an imitation of a semblance . . . **S**

003513

BEWILDERMENT. "So rational speculation leads to bewilderment [*hayra*] and theophany leads to bewilderment. There is nothing but a bewildered one. There is nothing exercising properties but bewilderment. There is nothing but Allah."[38] Bewilderment means

[38] Ibn al 'Arabi, *The Meccan Revelations*, ed. Michel Chodkiewicz, trans. William C. Chittick & James W. Morris (New York: Pir Press, 2005), 198.2. Chittick explicates the concept: "To find God is to fall into bewilderment (*hayra*), not the bewilderment of being lost and unable to find one's way, but the bewilderment of finding and knowing God and of not-finding and not-knowing Him at the same time. Every existent thing other than God dwells in a never-never land of affirmation and negation, finding and losing, knowing and not-knowing. The difference between the Finders and the rest of us is that they are fully aware of their own ambiguous situation. They know the significance of the saying of the first caliph Abū Bakr: 'Incapacity to

perplexity as a not-knowing-where-one-is-going/not-knowing-where-to-go that never stops moving, in any direction, or without direction, or in a direction that cannot be decided, a direction that might be either, but is absolutely neither, right or wrong: a direction that is pure direction and not direction at all.[39] Beyond *from* and *to*,[40] bewilderment relocates movement, making it "the omnipresent term of equation between anywhere and everywhere."[41] "The term *hayra* (perplexity) often renders *aporia* in Arabic translations from Greek. *Aporia* means that no passage (*poros*) has been found to the solution of a puzzle or impasse."[42] Bewilderment is the unfinishably perfect perpetuation of aporia's stalling, the pure anti-freezing of impasse into a plenitude of beautiful procession and flow. "Water. Millions of decaliters. A treasure. Greater than treasure, Usul. We have thousands of such caches, and only a few of us know them all. And when we have enough, we shall change the face of Arrakis."[43] Bewilderment is the mood of ultimate architecture: totalitarian porosity. All is passage, every way is the way because "*the* way after

---

attain comprehension is itself comprehension"' (William C. Chittick, *The Sufi Path of Knowledge: Ibn al-'Arabi's Metaphysics of Imagination* [Albany: State University of New York Press, 1989], 3-4).

[39] Counterpoint: Dante's Belacqua, who stays still precisely by knowing where he must go: "O frate, andar in sù che porta? . . . Prima convien che tanto il ciel m'aggiri / di fuor da essa, quanto fece in vita, / per ch'io 'ndugiai al fine I buon sospiri" (*Purgatorio* 4.127-32) [O brother, what's the use of going up? . . . First must the heavens revolve around me outside it, so long as they did during my life, because I delayed good sighs until the end]. Sloth's contrapasso is the self-imprisonment of being a profane *qutub*.

[40] "For the bewildered one has a round [*dawr*] / and a circular motion around the *qutb* / which he never leaves / But the master of the long path / tends away from what he aims for / seeking what he is already in / A master of fantasies which are his goal / He has a 'from' and a 'to' / and what is between them / But the master of the circular movement / has no starting point / that 'from' should take him over / and no goal / that he should be ruled by 'to' / He has the more complete existence / And is given the totality of the words and wisdoms" (Ibn Arabi, *Fusus al-hikam* [Bezels of Wisdom], chapter 3, cited from Michael Sells, *Mystical Languages of Unsaying*, 101-2).

[41] Nicola Masciandaro, "Becoming Spice: Commentary as Geophilosophy," *Collapse VI: Geo/Philosophy* (2010): 31.

[42] Joel L. Kraemer, "Maimondes, The Great Healer," *Maimonidean Studies* 5 (2008): 10.

[43] David Lynch, *Dune* (Universal Pictures, 1984).

all–it does not exist!"[44] All is process, the perpetual flashing of unending interstitial interchange between problem and solution, branch and intersection. "This conjunction [and] carries enough force to shake and uproot the verb 'to be.' Where are you going? Where are you coming from? What are you heading for? These are totally useless questions."[45] Follow me![46] This is the only way of staying with the center: constantly succeed to the furthest boundary of its infinite outside.[47] The motional essence of bewilderment–on this point the English etymology is ideally confused[48]–is captured in the unspelled difference between *hayra* and *hira* (whirlpool).[49] This image likewise locates you at the fountal threshold between spectatorship

---

[44] Friedrich Nietzsche, *Thus Spoke Zarathustra*, trans. Adrian del Caro (Cambridge: Cambridge University Press, 2006), 156.

[45] Gilles Deleuze and Félix Guattari, *A Thousand Plateaus: Capitalism and Schizophrenia*, trans. Brian Massumi (Minneapolis: University of Minnesota Press, 1987), 25.

[46] ". . . Swaying drunkenly to and fro like the branches, fresh as raw silk, which the winds have bent. *Gloss*: 'Swaying drunkenly,' in reference to the station of bewilderment (حيرة)" (Ibn Arabi, *Tarjuman al-Ashwaq* [Interpreter of Desires], trans. Reynold A. Nicholson [London: Royal Asiatic Society, 1911], 22.13).

[47] "That bewilderment is achieved in the continual transformation from form to form and in the circular motion beyond the dualism of origin and goal" (Sells, *Mystical Languages of Unsaying*, 102).

[48] According to the OED: from *wilder*, meaning "to cause to lose one's way, as in a wild or unknown place," "of uncertain origin: prob. (by an unusual process) extracted from *wilderness* on the analogy of the form of *wander*)." I.e. *wilder* turned *wilderness* into a verb on the motional model of *wander*.

[49] "'The [Universal] Order is perplexity, and perplexity is agitation and movement, and movement is life' [*al-'amr ḥīra wa-l-ḥīra qalaq wa ḥaraka wa-l-ḥaraka ḥayāt*]. I read the Arabic word حيرة here as *ḥīra* not *ḥayra* following Ibn 'Arabī's intention to identify 'perplexity' and 'whirlpool'. حيرة 'perplexity' can be read as *ḥīra* not *ḥayra*, Arabic dictionaries tell us, and 'whirlpool' (*ḥīra*) is one of the favourite images of universal life and order in Ibn 'Arabī's texts. The *ḥā'ir* 'perplexed' human being finds himself in constant movement. He cannot gain a foothold at any point, he is not established anywhere. This is why Ibn 'Arabī says that he is 'perplexed *in* the multiplication of the One': this 'multiplication' is not just epistemological, it is ontological as well, and the perplexed human being is moving in the whirlpool of life and cosmic Order and at the same time realises that he is at that movement" (Andrey Smirnov, "Sufi Hayra and Islamic Art: Contemplating Ornament through *Fusus al-Hikam*," paper presented at *Sufism, Gnosis, Art: The Thought of Ibn Arabi and Shah Nimatullah* [Seville, 22-23 November 2004]).

and existence. Not his drawable face, but something like this is what Narcissus really sees, an object of supreme confusion between image and self, line and substance. Only by standing over here, on this side beneath impassible overhanging barriers, does the eight-sided star convexly dip to kiss my crown.[50] Simultaneously, these marbly horizontals are absolutely steps that I am walking down, into the drowning death of living.[51] Image, dESIRE, is the guide: "guidance means being guided to bewilderment, that he might know the whole affair is perplexity, which means perturbation and flux, and flux is life."[52]

[50] "The Cosmos is like a net which takes all its life, as far as ever it stretches, from being wet in the water; it is at the mercy of the sea which spreads out, taking the net with it just so far as it will go, for no mesh of it can strain beyond its set place: the Soul is of so far-reaching a nature–a thing unbounded–as to embrace the entire body of the All in the one extension; so far as the universe extends, there soul is" (Plotinus, *Enneads*, 4.3.9).

[51] "For if anyone follow what is like a beautiful shape playing over water–is there not a myth telling in symbol of such a dupe, how he sank into the depths of the current and was swept away to nothingness? So too, one that is held by material beauty and will not break free shall be precipitated, not in body but in Soul, down to the dark depths loathed of the Intellective-Being, where, blind even in the Lower-World, he shall have commerce only with shadows, there as here" (Plotinus, *Enneads*, 1.6.7).

[52] Ibn Arabi, *Bezels of Wisdom* [Fusus al-Hikam], trans. R.W.J. Austin (New York: Paulist Press, 1980), 254.

Kristen Alvanson (born 1969, Minneapolis) is an American artist based in Iran and Malaysia. She attended The Cooper Union for the Advancement of Science and Art in New York and holds a degree from Sarah Lawrence College. She has participated in group/solo shows in New York, Tehran, London, Istanbul, Berlin, Belgium, Zürich and Vilnius including a solo exhibition of her work at Azad Gallery in Tehran and participation in the International Roaming Biennial of Tehran. Her writing and artworks have been published in *Collapse: Journal of Philosophical Research and Development*, *New Humanist*, *Frozen Tears III*, *Cabinet*, *Specialten* and *ITCH* Magazine. For more information visit Alvanson's website at www.kristenalvanson.com or her photoblog at <http://lumpen-orientalism.blogspot.com>. She has a forthcoming solo exhibition on her Women and Textiles Photography series in Tehran (2011) and is presently working on a book entitled *Lessons in Schizophrenia.*

Nicola Masciandaro is Associate Professor of English at Brooklyn College, The City University of New York. He is the author of *The Voice of the Hammer: The Meaning of Work in Middle English Literature* (Notre Dame, 2007) and essays on a variety of topics (beheading, the hand, commentary, mysticism, black metal, individuation, labor, Aesop, deixis, and Dante). Current projects include: *The Sorrow of Being*, *Speculative Medievalisms*, and *Spontaneity: A Commentary.*

Scott Wilson is Professor of Cultural Theory in the London Graduate School and the School of Humanities, Kingston University. His two most recent books are: *The Order of Joy: Beyond the Cultural Politics of Enjoyment* (SUNY Press, 2008) and *Great Satan's rage: American negativity and rap / metal in the age of supercapitalism* (Manchester University Press, 2008). He is co-editor (with Michael Dillon) of the *Journal for Cultural Research* (Taylor & Francis).

Glossator publishes original commentaries, editions and translations of commentaries, and essays and articles relating to the theory and history of commentary, glossing, and marginalia. The journal aims to encourage the practice of commentary as a creative form of intellectual work and to provide a forum for dialogue and reflection on the past, present, and future of this ancient genre of writing. By aligning itself, not with any particular discipline, but with a particular mode of production, Glossator gives expression to the fact that praxis founds theory.

GLOSSATOR.ORG

FORTHCOMING VOLUMES

Occitan Poetry

Volume Editors: Anna Kłosowska & Valerie Wilhite
Spring 2011

Contributiors: Michelle Bolduc, Bill Burgwinkle, Miriam Cabre, Marion Coderch, Charles Fantazzi, Virginie Greene, Cary Howie, Erin Labbie, Deborah Lyons, Simone Marchesi, Daniel O'Sullivan, Vincent Pollina, Isabel de Riquer Permanyer, Jean-Jacques Poucel, Wendy Pfeffer, Levente Selaf, Simo, Jesús Rodríguez-Velasco, Mark Taylor, Luke Sunderland, Valerie Wilhite.

On the Love of Commentary (in Love and Online)

Volume Editors: Nicola Masciandaro & Scott Wilson
Fall 2011

Contributors: Matthew Abbot, Eileen Joy, Karmen MacKendrick, Anna Kłosowska, Michael Moore, Jordan Kirk, Gary J. Shipley.

Black Metal

Volume Editors: Nicola Masciandaro & Reza Negarestani
Spring 2012

Contributors: Lee Barron, Ray Brassier, Henry Erik Butler, Dominic Fox, Manabrata Guha, Nicola Masciandaro, Reza Negarestani, Benjamin Noys, Zachary Price, Steven Shakespeare, Aspasia Stephanou, Eugene Thacker, James Trafford, Scott Wilson, Alex Williams, Evan Calder Williams, Ben Woodard.

Derrida's *The Post Card*

Volume Editor: Michael O' Rourke
Fall 2012

The Mystical Text: Black Clouds Course Through Me Unending . . .

Volume Editors: Nicola Masciandaro & Eugene Thacker
Spring 2013

Contributors: Ron Broglio, Kevin Hart, Karmen MacKendrick.

CPSIA information can be obtained at www.ICGtesting.com
Printed in the USA
LVOW01s1801260115

424408LV00036B/2526/P